"There is no more lovin grandparent to the chilaicn cmc one is wiser or stronger than Grandpa. No heart is more loving, or lap quite so cozy, as Grandma's. Nothing is closer to the heart of God or more central to the priorities of His Kingdom than the calling of bringing the little ones to Him. And nobody can do it quite like you, through your unique relationship—this book shows you how!"

—Dr. Wess Stafford, president emeritus, Compassion International, and author of *Too Small to Ignore: Why the Least of These Matter Most* and *Just a Minute: In the Heart of a Child, One Moment Can Last Forever*

"One of the questions I often receive from grandparents is 'Do you have a good resource with lots of practical ideas for how to be intentional grandparents?' Well, now we do. In this book, Josh, Jen, and Linda offer you a bounty of rich ideas any grandparent can do. Now that this book is in print, there are no excuses, Grandma and Grandpa. This is a treasure trove of ideas that will revolutionize how you grandparent and the impact you will have on your grandchildren. I can't wait to see the fruit that comes from grandparents putting these ideas into practice."

—Cavin Harper, founder, Christian Grandparenting Network

Discipling Your Grandchildren is timed perfectly—just as those of us in the baby boomer generation are struggling to learn how best to grandparent, a prophetic voice from Generation X is rising up and calling us to be more than occasionally "there." Dr. Josh Mulvihill's strong biblical foundation and groundbreaking research makes this book *the* thought leader in Christian grandparenting today. Every one of the 30 million Christian grandparents in America should have a copy of this inspiring book in their homes. Every church should have it available in their library. *Discipling Your Grandchildren* should be preached from our pulpits, read in our small groups, gratefully taken to heart, and then acted upon. I highly recommend this awesome book.

—Valerie Bell, Awana CEO

"You love your grandkids. Obviously! This book will help turn your love into Gospel-driven action. God has chosen you to be a grandparent for a reason. He has a call on your life to help those precious ones to know, love, and follow Jesus. The book you hold in your hands right now will equip you, encourage you, and give you practical ways to build strong relationships with your grandkids so that they might build strong relationships with God."

—Dr. Rob Rienow, founder, Visionary Family Ministries, www.VisionaryFam.com

"*Discipling Your Grandchildren* provides a valuable and practical blueprint, is easy to follow, full of wisdom, and includes a multitude of activities that will forever impact your relationship with your grandchildren, and together your relationship in Christ. It is a 'must read' for intentional Christian grandparents. Your life and the lives of your grandchildren will be truly blessed! The activities, which correspond to carrying out our mission as grandparents, are clearly mapped out and provide a broad approach to engage grandchildren and great-grandchildren of all ages. There is nothing this comprehensive available. The creative and easily understood activities identified throughout the book will impact how grandparents truly become intentional Christian grandparents."

—Dr. Vicki L. Rueckert, grandparent, educator, and Timberline Grandparent Ministries Director

"I often receive emails from grandparents who are seeking advice on how to be a stronger spiritual influence in the lives of their grandkids. I always point them to Josh Mulvihill's excellent resources! *Discipling Your Grandchildren* in particular is a virtual treasure trove of godly and practical ideas for creating a deeper spiritual connection with grandchildren. If you sometimes find yourself wondering what more you can do to help your grandkids know and love the Lord, this is *the* book you need!"

—Natasha Crain, national speaker, blogger, and author of *Keeping Your Kids on God's Side* and *Talking with Your Kids about Jesus*

"Are you looking for practical ideas on how to be more intentional in impacting your grandchildren for God's glory and their good? *Discipling Your Grandchildren* is an open treasure box, inviting grandparents to reach in for creative ways to nurture their relationships with the next generations for the sake of the Christ. Your children and grandchildren will be thankful that you've read this book and applied its God-honoring, Gospel-motivated ideas. Enjoy!"

—Larry E. McCall, author of *Grandparenting with Grace: Living the Gospel with the Next Generation*

Titles in the
GRANDPARENTING MATTERS
Series

DISCIPLING
YOUR
Grandchildren

Great Ideas to Help Them Know, Love, and Serve God

DR. JOSH MULVIHILL

WITH JEN MULVIHILL AND LINDA WEDDLE

BETHANYHOUSE
a division of Baker Publishing Group
Minneapolis, Minnesota

Published by Bethany House Publishers
11400 Hampshire Avenue South
Bloomington, Minnesota 55438
www.bethanyhouse.com

Bethany House Publishers is a division of
Baker Publishing Group, Grand Rapids, Michigan

Printed in the United States of America

ISBN 978-0-7642-3129-2

Library of Congress Control Number: 2019953220

Cover design by Dan Pitts

Josh Mulvihill is represented by William Denzel.

20 21 22 23 24 25 26   7 6 5 4 3 2 1

CONTENTS

FOREWORD

It was the death of a saint. As my family sorted through my grandma's little apartment, I came upon a book. It was Grandma Mason's well-worn Bible, old and tattered—verses underlined, thoughts scribbled in the margins, page corners folded down to mark tear-stained favorite passages. It sat on the table beside her rocking chair. The oak floor was grooved from years of rocking in that one place. The tabletop's finish had long since been rubbed off by her repeatedly reaching out to pull that cherished book to her lap. How fondly I remembered that a grandma's lap is like none other in the world.

Inside the brittle, cracked cover were pages of notes written by an obviously unsteady hand. Among others, there were decades-old papers marked "Prayers for Wess." I am the son of her daughter Marge and son-in-law Ken, who were missionaries in West Africa. Grandma's prayers for me traced my childhood in Africa and chronicled my every sickness, sorrow, and success, right up to my becoming president of Compassion International in 1993, just before her death. Through tear-brimmed eyes, I read the story of my life as told through Grandma's heartfelt prayers. I had never seen them before, and she never spoke of them, but I came to realize that my life's path—every challenge and choice, every struggle and victory—had been hidden in my Grandma's heart and poured out in prayer daily before her precious Lord.

Being a grandparent is not only a great privilege, it's a sacred mission. Whether your grandchildren live a world away in an African village or right next door, you have a calling that is an opportunity to change the world for your grandchildren, and even through your grandchildren. Nobody can take your particular, special place, and through your love, faith, guidance, and blessing poured into your grandchildren, they, and the world, can be blessed for eternity.

In my world travels with Compassion International, I rejoice when I see communities where the extended family is still intact and the whole village joins together to raise the children. In such places, grandparents play a natural and strategic role in the life of a family. Far from being marginalized, they are at the very center of village life. The older they become, the more they are respected and revered. Their wisdom and experience are valued, and they are called upon to pour into the next generations. Their children and grandchildren then return that love and care as their elders age and eventually need attention themselves. I know, for I grew up in such a place.

Can that loving, full-circle dynamic take place in the Western world of today? I am convinced it can. I've seen it, and you hold in your hands a strategic and creative guide to bring it about in your life as a grandparent, or as a parent who wants to more fully invite Grandma and Grandpa into the life of your son or daughter. God never intended for parents to go it alone. Being a loving grandparent is a relationship at the very heart of discipleship!

In my book *Just a Minute*, I make the point that the spirit of a child is soft and pliable, like moist clay. It takes "just a minute" and very little effort to make an impression on a child's life that could then set and last for eternity. As Graham Greene said, "There is always one moment in childhood when the door opens and lets the future in." If God places a child in your path for even one moment, it may well be a divine appointment. As a grandparent, you might be the one who says or does the right thing at the right time to launch the life of your grandchild. For my book, I asked people, "Who believed in you before you believed in yourself?" Time and again, the answer, whispered through tears, was, "It was my grandpa," or "It was my grandma." Much of the book could have been stories of grandparent heroes. Like you.

My prayer is that as a parent or grandparent, you will devour this important book cover to cover (or as I did, jump about from topic to topic, idea to creative idea) and prayerfully resolve to be actively involved in the little lives God has entrusted to you in your unique role. What an amazing opportunity we have to joyfully invest in this calling! May God bless you as you bless the children of your family and His Kingdom.

—Dr. Wess Stafford
President Emeritus, Compassion International
author of *Too Small to Ignore: Why the Least of These Matter Most* and *Just a Minute: In the Heart of a Child, One Moment Can Last Forever*

INTRODUCTION

Grandparenting is an incredible privilege and a serious responsibility. We hope this book helps you gain a new vision for the important role God has given grandparents and that it encourages you to make a commitment to actively and intentionally disciple your family. Every grandchild will live forever in heaven or hell, and we must not lose sight of this fact. Grandparenting in light of eternity helps us eliminate the vanities from life and focus on what matters most. Grandparents have a God-designed role discipling children and grandchildren. This book will help you fulfill that purpose. We wrote it to provide ideas to help you intentionally pass on to your family a heritage of faith in Christ.

What Makes This Book Unique?

It is written by a man and two women. Men and women grandparent differently, so having both perspectives is helpful. Grandfathers tend to gravitate toward activity and adventure that includes a ball, a tool, or danger. Grandmothers tend to gravitate toward a conversation over coffee, cooking together, or a shopping trip. Of course, these are generalities, so they may not fit your personality or preference. But that is why it is helpful to have the perspective of both men and women in these pages. There is something for everyone in this book.

It is grandparent tested and parent approved. Discipling Your Grandchildren was written by a grandparent and two parents. Understandably, books about grandparenting generally are written by grandparents for grandparents and rarely include the perspective of adult children. I'm not minimizing the value of these books. Many of them are written by friends and are great books. However, grandparenting is multigenerational. It relies heavily upon the cooperation and permission of adult children. Gaining the perspective of grandparents about grandparenting is needed, but it is only fifty percent of the equation. Grandparents know that you can only do what your adult children allow you to do with grandchildren. In the day of the autonomous individual, grandparenting restrictions are the ugly underbelly of grandparenting and the great frustration of many godly grandparents who want to invest more deeply with their family. That is why this book is unique. The ideas in it are not new to us; they have been implemented in our families and homes. They are grandparent tested, parent approved.

It is biblically based and application oriented. Discipling Your Grandchildren is the seventh book in the GRANDPARENTING MAT-TERS series with Bethany House Publishers. This book builds on the robust biblical foundation of *Grandparenting* and the scientific research of *Biblical Grandparenting*, which were the result of multiple years of PhD study. *Discipling Your Grandchildren* augments the other books in the series, with the goal of helping you apply discipleship to everyday life.

Meet the Authors

Discipling Your Grandchildren is written by three authors, each with different perspectives, life experiences, and strengths.

Linda Weddle has a degree in Christian education and is a certified early childhood educator. She has written thirteen books, including *How to Raise a Modern-Day Joseph*, and more than 2,000 short stories, articles, devotionals, and radio scripts for Christian organizations. For twenty-five years she worked at Awana as senior writer and program developer and taught workshops across the country. Since she was a teen, Linda has worked in just about every area of children's ministry, including many summers when she and her pastor husband team-taught at various camps. The camps gave her the opportunity to do one of her favorite things—tell stories to children that reflected their everyday lives, and in doing so, teach them biblical truths. Linda has two children, both serving in ministry, and six grandchildren. She has a blog for teachers and parents that can be found at groundthemforlife.com.

Jen Mulvihill is a music teacher and homeschool mom to five children. She is married to Josh, and together they are passionate about training children and families to know and love Jesus Christ. Jen considers it a privilege to be able to spend her days at home as a support to her husband and children. In her spare time, Jen can be found leading the homeschool band, which she launched in 2015, sewing, tending to her chickens and farm cats, and tackling a DIY project at their hundred-year-old farmhouse in Victoria, Minnesota. Jen's favorite things include growing deeper in relationship with her Lord and Savior Jesus Christ, encouraging other moms in the trenches of parenting, and laughing out loud with good friends over coffee.

Josh Mulvihill serves as the executive director of church and family ministry at Renewanation, where he equips parents and grandparents to disciple their family and coaches church leaders in children, youth, and family ministry with a focus on biblical worldview. He is the author or editor of seven books on grandparenting, including *Biblical Grandparenting* and *Grandparenting*, as well as the author of *Preparing Children for Marriage* and *Biblical Worldview*. Josh helped launch the Legacy Coalition, provides leadership to the Christian Grandparenting Network, and serves on the board of Awana. He was a pastor for nearly twenty years and has a PhD in family ministry from The Southern

Baptist Theological Seminary, where he did his dissertation on Christian grandparenting. Josh's primary ministry, and greatest joy, is being a husband and father. Josh is married to Jen, his college sweetheart, and they are blessed with five children. You can find Josh on the web at GospelShapedFamily.com.

Why Did We Write This Book?

To help grandparents prioritize the spiritual growth of grandchildren. A few years ago I (Josh) had the privilege of interviewing Christian grandparents all over America about their role as a grandparent as part of my PhD dissertation. I discovered that many Christian grandparents desire to help grandchildren grow in Christlike maturity, but there is a disconnect between stated priorities and the way grandparents use time with their grandchildren. I found that grandparents spoke about the importance of the spiritual growth of grandchildren; however, it commonly was not reflected in how they operated as a grandparent, revealing that the spiritual life of a grandchild was not as important as they claimed. We've written this book to help grandparents align their grandparenting practices with stated spiritual priorities and biblical principles. This book will help you prioritize the discipleship of children and grandchildren and make the most of every opportunity you have to shape faith and teach biblical truth so that your family knows, loves, and serves Christ.

To encourage grandparents to partner with parents to disciple children. Grandparents are needed more than ever. Raising children to know, love, and serve Jesus in today's secularized culture is a daunting task. Children need the intimate influence of as many godly individuals as possible in their life. Parents never were meant to bear the full weight of raising children. They are given the primary role, but God created grandparents to partner with parents to raise children to lifelong faith in Christ. Grandparents strengthen families, provide a safe place, are a last line of defense, and offer godly wisdom that is often lacking in other places in a child's life. There are millions of Christian grandparents in the United States. With a biblical vision and resources, we can transform families, churches, and society.

To equip grandparents to apply biblical principles about grandparenting. More than ever, families need to know what the Bible teaches about grandparenting and put it into practice. You won't find a formula for grandparenting in this book. We will not provide pragmatic approaches encouraging you to find what works for you. Our goal is greater than helping you become the cool grandparent and have fun with your family. Our ideas have a greater purpose. We wrote this book to help you apply the biblical methods of family discipleship from Deuteronomy 6 in everyday life.

Biblical Methods to Disciple Children

In the book *Grandparenting*, I explore eight biblical methods of discipleship for grandparents, which I will briefly introduce you to because the ideas in this book provide ways to implement these methods. Familiarize yourself with them so that there is context around why we emphasized certain topics or chose specific ideas for this book.

Asking questions. A key biblical method for growing the faith of future generations is question asking. Use questions to create serious spiritual dialogue, build a strong relationship, and discover what grandchildren believe. The spiritual practice of question asking is seen regularly in the Old and New Testaments. God commanded families in the Old Testament to practice traditions, eat specific foods, and erect stone pillars for the purpose of generating curiosity so that young people would ask questions that would encourage spiritual growth. Jesus mastered the art of asking good questions and used this method regularly.

Blessing. A spoken blessing is an opportunity for a grandparent to share his or her deep affection and desired future for a grandchild. A blessing is valuable because it creates a time and way to communicate affection and affirmation. Scripturally, we see blessings modeled by God as a common practice in the Old Testament and a repeated pattern of Scripture.

Intentional meals. God commands parents and grandparents to commit wholeheartedly to teaching the truths of God's Word to future generations and to "talk of them when you sit in your house" (Deuteronomy 6:7). What better place to practice "when you sit in your house" than around the table? A quick glance through Scripture reveals the value of food in the homes of God's people as a means to strengthen family relationships, celebrate God's provision, and as an opportunity to teach the Bible.

Prayer. God has given grandparents a solution to problems and challenging family situations. It's found in Philippians 4:6: "Do not be anxious about anything, but in everything by prayer and supplication with thanksgiving let your requests be made known to God." Prayer is the greatest answer. It is the first line of defense. Prayer is a wonderful gift to grandparents and an essential method to reach and disciple your family.

Communicating wisdom. A recurring theme from the book of Proverbs is that young people are prone to making poor choices and need the guidance of older, more mature believers (Proverbs 7:7). Proverbs teaches that young people need wisdom for everyday decisions such as choosing godly friends, sexual purity, honoring God with money, and a strong work ethic. The wise man in Proverbs 4:5 says to the young person, "Get wisdom; get insight." God has placed grandparents in the lives of grandchildren to help them make wise decisions. In order to do that, grandparents must know God's Word and know their grandchildren.

Reading and discussing the Bible. God instructs grandparents to teach grandchildren the truths of Scripture. Deuteronomy 4:9 (AMPC) states, "Teach them to your children and your children's children." In Psalm 78:5–6, God commands grandparents to teach multiple generations to obey God's commands. Throughout church history the primary method for teaching and discipling young people has been called family worship. Family worship is the means of introducing children to the truths of Scripture and preparing them for the Christian life. The practice consists of reading the Bible as a family, prayer, and praising God through music. *Telling God-stories.* In Psalm 78, God instructs older generations to tell younger generations about the work of God and His nature so that young people set their hope in God and keep His commands. One method of discipling grandchildren is to provide a testimony of God's work in our life through provision, conversion, and His countless blessings. The Bible utilizes this method to encourage future generations to praise God: "Let this be recorded for a generation to come, so that a people yet to be created may praise the Lord" (Psalm 102:18).

Sharing the Gospel. God places the responsibility of communicating the Gospel on all Christians, and this is true for grandparents with grandchildren. Children benefit from hearing the Gospel again and again from many sources. Children need to hear the good news of Christ's life, death, and resurrection at every age and stage. There is no such thing as hearing the Gospel too often, as children are prone to forget the Good News and be captivated by a gospel replacement. The child who hears the Gospel from parents and grandparents is blessed.

What Is Discipleship?

Jesus defined discipleship in two words: "Follow me." A disciple is a learner whose goal is to become like Jesus in character and help others do the same. Discipleship is the entire process of coming to faith and growing in spiritual maturity as a follower of Christ.

Discipleship is an invitation to orient our affections, thinking, and actions to align with God's. Discipleship is the process by which an individual who has received new life takes on the character of Jesus and commits to living in obedience to God's commands. What we love, how we think, and how we live are all components of discipleship.

Paul's list in 2 Timothy 3:10–11 is a multifaceted picture of discipleship. Paul states, "You . . . followed my teaching, my conduct, my aim in life, my faith, my patience, my love, my steadfastness, my persecutions and sufferings." We can generally measure discipleship by assessing these areas of our life and the lives of our children and grandchildren.

- *Conduct*: Can we say to our children and grandchildren, "Imitate me as I imitate Christ?" Do we have anything to hide?
- *Character*: Do we practice what we preach? How are we displaying the fruit of the Spirit in our home?
- *Teaching*: Do we teach Christ crucified and the whole counsel of the Word of God?
- *Purpose*: Are we living a life of self-indulgence, or a life of service to Jesus?
- *Suffering*: What is our demeanor when we face a trial?

We hope this book helps you intentionally disciple your family. Intentionality means *action by design*. It is the preplanned implementation of God's instruction. Intentionality involves an understanding of desired outcomes and an awareness to look for opportunities toward that end.

Overview of the Book

Discipling Your Grandchildren is organized around eleven topics that most grandparents experience with children and grandchildren. There are ninety-six different sections, with hundreds of ideas designed to help you be an intentional disciple-making grandparent. Each chapter contains a list of ideas, concisely explained, often in bullet-point format. We want to provide as many ideas as possible, so you won't find an introduction to each chapter. We jump right in with an idea.

The ideas in this book are not random or purposeless. They are a means to a greater end. Of course, disconnected from the biblical purpose of discipleship, they become just another activity with a grandchild. We encourage you to read the ideas with discipleship in mind and utilize them toward that end. There are two ways *Discipling Your Grandchildren* can be read. Read it from beginning to end, or skip around and use it as a reference tool. However you utilize this book, we hope it is one that you will come back to again and again. Feel free to mark it up, dog-ear pages, and keep notes about which ideas you have implemented with each set of grandchildren.

It is our prayer that God will work through you to bless your family with a heritage of faith in Christ that lasts for generations to come. We hope this book helps you disciple your children's children and build strong family relationships that bring glory to God and impact the world for Christ. If you are a grandparent, then God has called you to the ministry of grandparenting. May you joyfully commit to this important task and faithfully invest in discipling your family.

1

What Does the Bible Say about Grandparenting?

Five Characteristics
of a Disciple-Making Grandparent

Christian grandparents need to take a few moments to ask, "What does the Bible say about grandparenting?" "What is the goal?" "What am I trying to accomplish in the lives of my children and grandchildren?" For many Christian grandparents, the answer is to be a loving friend, an encouraging voice, or a supportive help. These are all good things, but they are not the primary goal that God provides in the Bible.

Many parenting and family experts label their stuff as "Christian," but it is nothing more than secular ideas given a Christian veneer using biblical expressions and words. There are a growing number of books for grandparents, and many of them adopt the latest trends and buzzwords and try to blend them with Scripture. The resulting marriage produces bitter fruit.

There are also books on grandparenting that claim to be biblical, but are only loosely based on the Bible's teaching about grandparenting. Resources that disregard the clear teaching of the Bible about grandparenting for other sources provide the wrong kind of guidance. The best books focus on essential biblical principles, not the creation of a grandparenting model or system that works right out of the box. The result is a list of steps and how-tos that quickly supersedes the more important biblical principles.

What we desperately need is an understanding of the biblical principles of grandparenting and a commitment to obey God's Word in this area of life. If Christian grandparents consistently applied a few simple principles that are clearly communicated in God's Word, it would yield a far greater return for Christian grandparents than any revolutionary model or trendy method.

I have written extensively about the biblical principles of grandparenting in the books *Grandparenting* and *Biblical Grandparenting*, but I will provide a few principles here to provide a foundation for the ideas in this book and commend those books to you for additional reading.

Deuteronomy 6:1–9

The most common passage of Scripture utilized for family discipleship is Deuteronomy 6:4–9. The Christian community often limits the application of Deuteronomy 6 to parents, but based on the context of Deuteronomy 6:1–2, it has a broader application that includes grandparents. Moses gave the community a charge to love the Lord and diligently teach young people the commands of God. Moses states the commands of God are for "you and your son and your *son's son*" (Deuteronomy 6:1–2, emphasis added). The reference to "son's son" means that Deuteronomy 6:4–9 is not only for parents but also for grandparents. From a biblical perspective, grandparents have a critical role with the next generation that is centered around the transmission of faith.

Deuteronomy 6 helps us remember that discipleship is not one more thing to add to an already busy schedule. Discipleship is not a separate activity we do with a child. It is integrated into all of life. Discipleship can happen while playing catch, cooking dinner, watching a movie, driving in the car, reading the Bible, or working in the garden. According to Deuteronomy 6:7, the following portions of each day present great opportunities to disciple children:

- Mealtime: "when you sit in your house"
- Travel time: "when you walk by the way"
- Bedtime: "when you lie down"
- Morning time: "when you rise"

Discipleship is what we do as we go through our day. The biblical pattern is for the truth of the Bible to be transferred through everyday activity when we get ready for bed, eat a meal together, ride in the car, fold laundry together, engage in late-night talks, and have fun together. Grandparents who think that they can compartmentalize life by assigning a certain number of hours per week to spend on grandparenting have a philosophy that is contrary to the spirit of Deuteronomy 6. It is also a recipe to become a distant or disengaged grandparent. Most Christian grandparents I've met want to make an eternal difference in the lives of their children and grandchildren. The Bible tells us how to do that. Before we provide ideas to help you implement Deuteronomy 6 and disciple your grandchildren, let's examine a few biblical characteristics that lay the foundation to be a disciple-making grandparent.

Disciple-Making Grandparents View Grandchildren as a Blessing

The Bible clearly teaches that grandchildren are a blessing to be embraced, not a burden to be avoided. The Bible tells us that it is a blessing to *know* our grandchildren. Psalm 128:6 states, "May you see your children's children." The ministry of grandparenting is to be received as a blessing. The grandparent who has a poor attitude toward grandparenthood in general or a grandchild specifically is at odds with God's plan.

Every grandchild is created in the image of God and is therefore His sovereign plan for your life. Every grandchild is to be highly valued regardless of gender, race, health, or personality. Every grandchild is to be received with love and embraced as God's good design for your life. If you struggle to receive a grandchild as a blessing, pray that God would soften your heart and change your attitude. Ask God to give you His love for a grandchild. Some of us need to release our plans to the Lord and choose to trust God's sovereign plan for our life even when life turns out differently than envisioned.

We must allow the Bible to shape our view of grandchildren. The Bible tells us that it is a blessing to *have* grandchildren. Proverbs 17:6 states, "Grandchildren are the crown of the aged." That significant statement speaks to the incredible value of grandchildren. Interestingly, it is not wealth, health, career accomplishments, or social status that the Bible says are the crown of your life. That honor goes to grandchildren. A crown bestows honor and represents a high position in life. Your attitude and actions should reflect the value given to grandchildren by God in Scripture. Grandchildren are the blessing God has given you. Grandparenting gives life meaning. One sure way to experience misery is to neglect a blessing that God has given us. Grandchildren are a good gift from a good God who are to be embraced.

Disciple-Making Grandparents Understand the Biblical Purpose of Grandparenting

My research discovered that only about one in four Christian grandparents has clarity about the purpose of grandparenting. Many Christian grandparents operate as companions who emphasize emotional support or provide a helping hand but have a limited spiritual impact on family. A high percentage of Christian grandparents have unintentionally adopted an unbiblical role due to strong cultural messages, and the result is a disconnected family, loneliness, and overburdened children. If cultural messages are absorbed, then grandparents are placed at the periphery of family life where it is difficult to maintain close family relationships and significant discipleship of children and grandchildren. It is important to recognize and reject the cultural messages that encourage grandparents to live an independent life from family through noninterference and emotional autonomy as well as those that focus on indulgence of grandchildren by spoiling them and being their playmate. Discipleship is very difficult if independence and indulgence are central to one's grandparenting philosophy.

The Bible teaches that God designed grandparenting for the purpose of multigenerational family discipleship. Colossians 1:16 states, "All things were created through him and for him." Grandparenting was created by God and for God. This is an important point for all Christian grandparents to understand because everything God creates, including grandparenting, he creates for a reason. If God created grandparenting, the natural question that arises is why? God must have a purpose for it.

God designed the family as the first and most important means of discipling children. God created a multigenerational approach to discipleship, which includes two parents (a man and a woman) and four grandparents, as well as the church family. Due to divorce on demand, death, single-parent homes, and the sexual revolution, this picture is increasingly uncommon. Grandparents are God-designed teachers, models, mentors, shepherds, and sometimes surrogate parents who fill the gap created when brokenness touches our home. God gave you grandchildren so you can make disciples of all nations, beginning with your family. Discipleship is not easy work, but it is your purpose, and it is more satisfying than anything retirement can offer.

God created parents and grandparents as partners working toward the same goal, with different but complementary roles. Grandparents have been given a sacred trust in grandchildren,

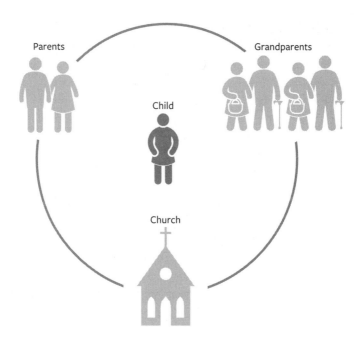

who are to be shepherded with care. Biblically, grandparents are disciple-makers who are to pass on a heritage of faith in Christ to future generations. Grandparents are fellow laborers created to point grandchildren to Christ and help raise them to spiritual maturity.

God designed parents as the primary disciple-makers in a child's life and He created grandparents as a secondary but important influence. If parents are raising children in the Lord, then grandparents support and encourage parents to fulfill the task God has given them and reinforce the work of the parent by investing directly into the spiritual life of a child and grandchild. In this case, you are discipling the disciple-makers. If parents are not raising children in the Lord, then grandparents need to lovingly encourage parents to take seriously the responsibility God has given them. Parents who are not actively discipling present an opportunity for grandparents to invest more heavily by stepping into a more prominent disciple-making role in the life of a grandchild.

Disciple-Making Grandparents Bear Spiritual Fruit

Psalm 92:12–15 paints the picture that we are to produce spiritual fruit for all of life. The psalmist uses the image of a palm tree to make his point: "The righteous will flourish like a palm tree, they will grow like a cedar of Lebanon; planted in the house of the Lord, they will flourish in the courts of our Lord. They will still bear fruit in old age, they will stay fresh and green, proclaiming, 'The Lord is upright; he is my Rock, and there is no wickedness in him'" (NIV).

Date palm trees bear hundreds of pounds of fruit well past 150 years of age and are a picture of what God expects from grandparents in the later third of their life. The psalmist teaches that righteousness in old age results in the continued production of spiritual fruit.

Psalm 92 shouts a truth that all grandparents need to hear: Age does not impair fruit-bearing capabilities. It enhances them. Psalm 92 reminds grandparents that the latter years of life ought to be spiritually productive years for the purpose of declaring the nature of God to others. American culture attempts to convince grandparents that you have little to offer. Nothing is further from the truth. This passage speaks against the American ethos of retirement and reminds grandparents to be fruitful disciple-makers to their dying day.

Grandparents need to reject the narrative that the purpose of old age is a life of leisure and self-indulgence. The example of the palm tree suggests that a fruitless existence is not a category the Bible recognizes. God's expectation for palm trees is also true for grandparents: To live is to bear fruit, even in old age.

Grandparenting fruit, in part, is measured by faithfulness to God's commands. If we measure success based on what grandchildren do or become, we have set ourselves up for disappointment. We can only control ourselves, not how our children or grandchildren respond. Sometimes children or grandchildren who grow up in good Christian homes abandon Christ. Other times, God graciously transforms the lives of grandchildren whose families were a mess and parents were failures. In general, grandparents who follow biblical principles will see a positive effect on their family. God uses faithful grandparents as instruments in the salvation and sanctification of family members' lives. However, a grandchild's salvation is a matter that is settled between them and God, so we must diligently commit to praying for and impressing the truths of the Bible on a grandchild's heart.

Disciple-Making Grandparents Focus on Their Own Spiritual Life

The Bible teaches that the first priority for a grandparent is *who* before *what*. God tells grandparents, "Only be careful, and watch yourselves closely so that you do not forget the things your eyes have seen or let them fade from your heart as long as you live. Teach them to your children and their children after them" (Deuteronomy 4:9 NIV). In *Grandparenting*, the following point is made:

> What we do is a result of who we are. The condition of your heart determines every aspect of your life, including what you do as a grandparent. That is why it is safe to say that grandparenting is a matter of the heart. Most writing on grandparenting focuses on methods. The idea is that if you aren't getting the right results, you must be doing the wrong things. But family literature that focuses on the external will never bring about lasting change. The starting place must be on your inner life—your thoughts, your motives, your values, and your beliefs.[1]

The Bible teaches that the real issues of life are spiritual and are matters of the heart. That's why God is concerned with *who* a grandparent is before *what* a grandparent does. Disciple-making grandparents, the ones who make an eternal difference, are those who are serious about their own spiritual condition by grieving over their own sin, hungering for Christ, and continuing to grow in spiritual maturity. Grandparents who passionately pursue Christ and live a God-honoring life present a strong apologetic that will not go unnoticed and will become a powerful instrument that God can use for the salvation of a grandchild.

God's command to watch ourselves closely has many implications. It is a call to be holy and live in obedience to God's commands. It suggests that our walk with Christ is the most important aspect of grandparenting. It is a reminder that no matter our age, our heart can grow cold and our affections can be misplaced. It is a warning not to make the same mistake as the Israelites, who forgot the work of God. It is an exhortation to fight the good fight of faith and finish the race strong.

Disciple-Making Grandparents Teach the Bible to Grandchildren

The Bible prioritizes teaching as the primary method of helping future generations know Christ and grow in maturity. Let's explore a few passages that command grandparents to teach the truth of God's Word to young people (emphases added):

- "*Teach* them to your children and to their children after them" (Deuteronomy 4:9 NIV).
- "Fear the Lord your God, you and your son and your sons' son. . . . You shall *teach* them diligently to your children, and shall *talk* about them when you sit . . . walk . . . lie down . . . rise" (Deuteronomy 6:2, 7).
- "He commanded our [fore] fathers to *teach* to their children, that the next generation might know them, the children yet unborn, and arise and tell them to their children" (Psalm 78:5–6).
- "Older women . . . are to *teach* what is good, and so train the young women to love their husbands and children, to be self-controlled, pure, working at home, kind, and submissive to their own husbands . . ." Older men, "*urge* the younger men to be self-controlled" (Titus 2:3–6).

33

Grandparents are to use the Bible to shape who a child becomes and how the child lives. This is the pattern and command of Scripture. Grandparents in Deuteronomy were commanded to teach the law of God (Ten Commandments) to children so that future generations would develop an understanding of right and wrong. Grandparents in the Psalms were given a mandate to tell future generations about God's character and His work, and to teach God's laws so that children would not rebel against God. The grandparents of Titus 2 shape future generations by providing character training and guidance about how to be a godly mother and wife.

There is no substitute for living in a manner worthy of the Gospel, but also let us commit to verbally teaching biblical truths to the next generation so that they may develop a deep, lasting, Scripture-rooted faith that makes a difference for Christ in the world.

Discipleship is a slow process of small interactions over the course of a long time. It doesn't feel spectacular to read the Bible for ten minutes with a grandchild or discuss matters of faith spontaneously for a few minutes, but over time the collective impact is significant. If you invest a mere thirty minutes a week to disciple a grandchild and do this from birth through eighteen years old, you will have invested 28,080 minutes (468 hours) discipling a grandchild.

God's method for growth is spectacularly slow. The massive oak tree in my yard has been growing for more than 150 years. It grows at a rate that is slow and indiscernible. The God who slowly grows a strong, beautiful oak tree is the same God who grows a child's faith. It is the ordinary opportunities and the biblical conversations, ten minutes at a time, week after week, that God uses to shape the hearts and minds of children. We may not see immediate results, but we can pray that God would use the moments to help a grandchild know, love, and serve Christ.

Let us avoid the temptation of instant discipleship or thinking that everything we do with a grandchild needs to be momentous and memorable. Some things will be. There should be some "wow" moments! But there will be many more mundane encounters. There is beauty in both. Whether momentous or mundane, I encourage a commitment to a long habit of reading the Bible, discussing it with a child, integrating God's Word into daily activities and interactions that you will find in this book, and intentionally capitalizing on the opportunities we have—of whatever frequency that may be. Spiritual maturity is fueled by everyday interactions with godly people. Some are planned and some are spontaneous. This book will help you capture those everyday opportunities to intentionally disciple your children and grandchildren.

2

Gifts, Encouragement, and Prayer

Gift Giving

Consider making a tradition of giving a practical gift children will use on a daily basis. You can make choosing the item part of the gift. Parents will appreciate that these items are not added to the family budget, and grandchildren will love the one-on-one time with you! Plan a day with grandma and grandpa to choose

- New shoes for a birthday
- Professional family photography
- School supplies or a backpack for school
- A winter coat
- Sports equipment for their extracurricular activity
- Fresh sheets and blankets for their bedroom
- Tools to teach biblical manhood or womanhood

Ten Graduation Gift Ideas

Be creative and share your faith heritage through your gift giving this graduation season. Above all, think memory with meaning. If possible, be there in person to celebrate with a grandchild.

1. Personalized photography: Frame a memorable event of the graduating grandchild—even better if you are in the photo together.

2. Overnight bag: Invite your grandchild to come see you, especially if he or she is going away to college.

3. Heirloom jewelry: Pass on a special piece to your college-bound grandchild and write a note that it is a reminder that you are with him or her.

4. An experience: Purchase tickets around what interests your grandchild, such as music or sports. Be creative. Continue to make memories, even as they grow older.

5. Talk time: Ask your grandchild to teach you how to use Skype, Marco Polo, or Zoom so you can stay in communication. Choose the method that works best for you.

6. Handwritten letter: Tell them you love them, are there for them, and will be praying for them during this next season of life. You may want to include specific Scriptures you will pray.

7. Scrapbook of memories: Create a book of photos and journal entries about what you did together.

8. Family memento: Share its meaning, when you received it, and why you are passing it on to your grandchild.

9. T-shirt quilt: Order or make a quilt using a grandchild's old T-shirts. You will need to collect these shirts from camp, school, and family trips. You can find a company online by Googling "T-shirt quilt." Send the company the T-shirts, and they do the rest.

10. Gift cards for gas, restaurants, clothing, or electronic stores where they shop.

The Gift of a Bible

Children begin to read fluently around second or third grade and are able to read the Bible on their own. We recommend giving your grandchild a children's Bible from their first days and a full-text Bible when they are around ten years old or older. It is a gift they will likely keep their entire lives. You will be able to engage the Scriptures with them on a deeper level by ensuring your grandchild has a Bible. As you give the gift of a Bible, consider doing one or more of the following:

- Select the translation that is most used in their church. If you're not sure which translation to purchase, ESV or NIV is a good choice.
- Give a Bible that has a hard or leather cover and sturdy binding.
- Look at multiple Bibles before selecting one. Some Bibles are geared toward children but will be too childish for a teen. Select a Bible they will be able to use for many years, into adulthood if possible.
- Give a cover with the Bible. A cover will protect it from water and dirt while also providing space to keep pens or study notes. If you sew, make a fun cover in indoor/outdoor fabric that is reflective of your grandchild's personal style.
- Add tabs. If the Bible you select doesn't have tabs built into the pages, consider whether or not you would like to add them. Most Christian bookstores sell black and white tabs. Look on Etsy for Bible tabs in unique feminine or masculine styles. Place the tabs on the correct pages prior to gifting the Bible. Younger children will not be able to

do this themselves, and it allows for Bible passages to be found quickly.

- Think through accessories! Archival pens, highlighters, and stickers make Bible study more of a creative experience.
- Write in the front of the Bible. Include the child's name, date, the occasion on which the Bible is being given, and a special verse or prayer.
- Prior to giving the Bible to your grandchild, take time to highlight or underline special passages of Scripture. These can include
  » If your grandchild has a biblical name, the passages where their name is mentioned
  » The story of creation
  » Psalm 23
  » Romans Road of Salvation: Romans 3:23; 6:23; 5:8; 10:9–10
  » Verses you have prayed specifically for them in the past
  » Any stories, chapters, or verses you would like to stand out for them

Connect through Texts

A great way to keep in contact with your grandchild is through text messages. Younger children won't have the capability to do this (unless dad or mom assists), but older children will often have access to a phone or tablet. A short word of encouragement can mean a lot to a child.

You will need a phone or device that allows you and your grandchild to connect. Remember that parents set the parameters for a child's use of such devices, not grandparents. Don't pressure the parents to purchase a device for a child or give electronics as a gift without the parents' permission.

If a grandchild has the ability to text, keep in contact with him or her by sending an occasional message. This could be a greeting, a joke, a verse of Scripture, or an encouraging word. Find out when a child has a tournament, a special event, or test and send a text such as, "I'm praying you'll do your very best today." Text after the event to find out how they did.

Five short and encouraging Bible verses to text to your grandchild before a big event or test:

1. "Have I not commanded you? Be strong and courageous. Do not be frightened, and do not be dismayed, for the Lord your God is with you wherever you go" (Joshua 1:9).
2. "Be strong, and let your heart take courage, all you who wait for the Lord!" (Psalm 31:24).
3. "Cast your burden on the Lord, and he will sustain you" (Psalm 55:22).
4. "Finally, be strong in the Lord and in the strength of his might" (Ephesians 6:10).
5. "Casting all your anxieties on him, because he cares for you" (1 Peter 5:7).

If you don't know how to text, this is a gentle encouragement to learn. Children communicate today through texts. You'll be more likely to get a child to answer a text than to answer a phone call, email, or letter. Texting can be a fun and great way to communicate. You can send your grandchild an unexpected message of encouragement, but you might also receive an unexpected message of encouragement from your grandchild that just might make your day.

Dos and don'ts of texting a grandchild:

- Don't send a barrage of texts. You want to be encouraging, not annoying.
- Do keep texts short.

- Do send pictures via text or Snapchat. These could be funny, an interesting place you're visiting, or a picture of a verse that means a lot to you.

- Don't scold for not texting back. Children are busy with activities and homework. Often parents set limitations on when they can use their devices, so they aren't on them all day.

- Do answer a child's text as soon as possible. You want to encourage her or him to text you back.

- Do read over your text before you send it. Autocorrect can insert things you didn't intend to say.

- Don't make plans with your grandchild unless you've first talked to the parents.

Build Your Grandchild's Library of Good Books

The opportunities to give gifts to grandchildren are endless. Starting with baby showers before they are born, up through adulthood, books are an excellent way to make connections and are discipleship tools. Consider the average toy given at a child's birthday party. A toy is played with and enjoyed for a season, but a good book will be read over and over again and kept for many years, often well beyond the child's reading level or listening age, because of the memories made by reading together, discussing the subject matter, and the desire to retain this treasure of lasting value.

When giving the gift of a good book, consider the following:

- Write a note to your grandchild on the inside cover noting the date of the gift and the significance. For example, "To Johnny at your baby shower. We can't wait to read this book to you! Love, Grammie and Pops."

- Keep a list of the books you have gifted so you don't give the same book twice.

- Communicate your desire to build your grandchild's library to your adult children. If finances allow, give your grandchild a well-made bookshelf to hold their books from you. Ask your adult children their style preference and even go shopping together to choose something that will be used for many years to come.
- Consider milestone books as gifts for all of your grandchildren. Include books that teach core biblical truth. If you have multiple grandchildren, buy these books in bulk and keep them on hand to give yearly or at milestones. For example:
  » Baby showers: *Jesus Storybook Bible*, *Pat the Bunny*, *Goodnight Moon*
  » First birthday: *The Big Picture Story Bible*, *First Bible Basics*, a Beatrix Potter collection
  » First Christmas: *The Christmas Promise* book with a Fisher-Price nativity set
  » Second birthday: LITTLE LIGHTS biographies, *The Biggest Story ABC*, *I Love You Through and Through*
  » Second Christmas: *The Legend of the Candy Cane*, *If He Had Not Come*
  » Third birthday: *The Bible in Pictures for Little Eyes*, *Right Choices*, *A Child's Garden of Verses*
- When possible, purchase hardcover editions of books. Hardcovers are more durable for little hands, stand better on bookcases, and provide a substantial place for writing to your grandchildren on the inside cover.
- For older children, a book with an accompanying related activity makes a wonderful gift. For example, give the LITTLE HOUSE series along with a note telling the child you will take them to visit a living farm from the 1800s. Or give a book with a gift card to an ice cream shop or bakery so you can discuss your favorite parts of the story.

- If your grandchildren do not like books, help them to see the value of a good book. Sit down and read to them beginning when they are very young. Reading a children's book doesn't take long, and grandchildren will learn to love snuggling on your lap and listening to your voice. As grandchildren get older, read them a chapter each week, and make it a standing date. Don't let distance deter you; take advantage of technology to read together via video or phone.

Books to Give and Enjoy Together

The Little Years:

I Love You Through and Through by Bernadette Rossetti-Shustak and Caroline Jayne Church

Board books by Sandra Boynton

Goodnight Moon by Margaret Wise Brown and Clement Hurd

Pat the Bunny by Dorothy Kunhardt and Golden Books

The Very Hungry Caterpillar by Eric Carle

The Jesus Storybook Bible by Sally Lloyd-Jones and Jago

Little Golden Books

The Big Picture Story Bible by David R. Helm and Gail Schoonmaker

The Biggest Story ABC by Kevin DeYoung and Don Clark

A Farmer's Alphabet by Mary Azarian

Everything a Child Should Know about God by Kenneth Taylor

The Bible in Pictures for Little Eyes by Kenneth Taylor

Right Choices by Kenneth Taylor

Brown Bear, Brown Bear, What Do You See? by Bill Martin Jr. and Eric Carle

First Bible Basics by Danielle Hitchen
The Beginners Gospel Story Bible by Jared Kennedy
The Garden, the Curtain and the Cross by Carl Laferton

Early Readers:

Learn-to-Read Bible by Heather Germmen
Books by Dr. Seuss
FROG AND TOAD series by Arnold Lobel
LITTLE TIM series by Edward Ardizzone

Biographies That Will Captivate:

LITTLE LIGHTS series by Catherine MacKenzie
HISTORY LIVES series by Mindy Withrow and Brandon Withrow
CHRISTIAN BIOGRAPHIES FOR YOUNG READERS series by Simonetta Carr
LIGHTKEEPERS FOR GIRLS series by Irene Howat
LIGHTKEEPERS FOR BOYS series by Irene Howat
LITTLE PEOPLE, BIG DREAMS series by Isabel Sanchez Vegara
JUNGLE DOCTOR series by Paul White
TRAILBLAZERS series by various authors
Books by Ingri and Edgar Parin D'Aulaire
The Church History ABCs by Stephen J. Nichols and Ned Bustard

Books That Will Be Read Again and Again:

LITTLE HOUSE series by Laura Ingalls Wilder
THE CHRONICLES OF NARNIA series by C. S. Lewis
WINGFEATHER SAGA series by Andrew Peterson
Contemporary fiction from Rabbit Room Press

Anything written by E. B. White

Teddy's Button by Amy LeFeuvre

THE MOFFATS series by Eleanor Estes

Treasure in an Oatmeal Box by Ken Gire

THE GREEN EMBER series by S. D. Smith

100 Cupboards by N .D. Wilson

A WRINKLE IN TIME series by Madeline L'Engle

Mary Poppins by P. L. Travers

Books by Beverly Clearly

The Door in the Wall by Marguerite de Angeli

GREAT ILLUSTRATED CLASSICS series by various authors

Strawberry Girl by Lois Lenski

Laddie (or anything) by Gene Stratton-Porter

THE LORD OF THE RINGS series by J. R. R. Tolkien

The Adventures of Tom Sawyer by Mark Twain

Heidi by Johanna Spyri

Twice Freed by Patricia St. John

WINNIE-THE-POOH series by A. A. Milne

ANNE OF GREEN GABLES series by L. M. Montgomery

Christmas:

A Christmas Carol by Charles Dickens

The Best Christmas Pageant Ever by Barbara Robinson

Behold the Lamb of God by Russ Ramsey

The Legend of the Candy Cane by Lori Walburg

If He Had Not Come by David Nicholson with endnotes by
    Josh Mulvihill

Prepare Him Room Advent Devotional by Marty Mechowski

The Christmas Miracle of Jonathan Toomey by Susan
    Wojciechowski

Christmas Memories Book by Lynn Anderson
I Saw Three Ships by Elizabeth Goudge

Poetry:

A Child's Garden of Verses by Robert Louis Stevenson
Poetry collections by Shel Silverstein

Adventure and Outdoors:

The Dangerous Book for Boys by Conn Iggulden and Hal
  Iggulden
The Daring Book for Girls by Andrea J. Buchanan and Mir-
  iam Peskowitz
The American Boy's Handy Book by Daniel Carter Beard
The Field and Forest Handy Book by Daniel Carter Beard
  and David R. Godin
Camp Out: The Ultimate Kids' Guide by Lynn Brunelle
Keeping a Nature Journal by Clare Walker Leslie and
  Charles E. Roth

Theology and Worldview:

My 1st Book of Questions and Answers by Carine
  Mackenzie
Resources from Answers in Genesis
Books, DVDs, and music by Buddy Davis
The Ology: Ancient Truths Ever New by Marty Machowski
The Radical Book for Kids by Champ Thornton
What Does the Bible Say About That? by Kevin Swanson
God's Names, God's Battles, God's Promises, God's Word
  books by Sally Michael
Holman Illustrated Bible Dictionary for Kids, Holman Refer-
  ence Editorial Staff

The Biggest Story: How the Snake Crusher Brings Us Back to the Garden, by Kevin DeYoung and Don Clark

Bible Study:

Exploring the Bible by David Murray
Long Story Short and *Old Story New* by Marty Machowski
Character Sketches by Institute in Basic Life Principles
Sermon Notes for Kids by Jill Connelly

Books about Books:

Honey for a Child's Heart by Gladys Hunt
The Read-Aloud Handbook by Jim Trelease
Books Children Love by Elizabeth Wilson
The Read-Aloud Family by Sarah Mackenzie

Giving Gifts of Experiences

Many children are overwhelmed with stuff, so give the gift of an adventure instead. Not only will you have a fun time together, but you'll also create a memory that won't be forgotten and you will develop a closer relationship, which will provide opportunities to spiritually nurture your grandchild's faith in Christ. Adventures work well for birthdays, because you can interact with the child one-on-one, rather than have all grandchildren involved. Even if you have twin grandchildren, do something individually with each child.

Use the drive time to have good conversations. Ask fun and serious questions such as:

- If you could go anywhere in the world, where would you go?
- What is your favorite Bible verse and why?
- If someone wrote a book about you, what should the book be called?

- What's the first question you want to ask when you get to heaven?
- If you had to teach the kids at church next Sunday, what would your lesson be about?

Where should you go and what can you do on your adventure? Here are some ideas:

- Eat at a special restaurant.
- Paint pottery.
- Attend the premiere of a Christian movie.
- Help at a food bank.
- Attend a play.
- Do an alphabet day. Don't return home until you do something starting with every letter of the alphabet, which includes buying small gifts for parents. That takes care of M for mom's gift and D for dad's. Buy a few bouquets of flowers and take them to a nursing home, where you can ask the receptionist to give them to neglected patients; then you can cross off F for flowers.
- Go on an overnight trip. Hike in a local park, go camping, or visit a museum. If your work allows, take a grandchild with you for a conference workshop where he or she can help distribute handouts, perform tasks, and serve as a business or ministry partner with you.
- Be alert to special events happening in your area. Ask other parents and grandparents where they've gone with their children or grandchildren. Ask your grandchildren where they'd like to go.
- Be creative and have an adventure! Remember, some parents limit when, where, and how much time grandparents can spend with grandchildren. The parents are the parents and always have the final say.

- Don't forget to think about anything a child might require for your adventure: car seat, diapers, snacks, warm jacket, picnic lunch, spending money, and camera.

Journaling Together

Co-writing a journal with your grandchildren is one way to connect on a consistent basis and be an encouragement to one another; it is also a tangible reminder of you and your words that a grandchild can keep for life. You will need to purchase a journal, and you might want to consider coloring pens to add some fun to the journal.

Start the journal by writing an introduction, including the date, and write the first entry. Consider adding your grandchild's grade, any activities he or she is in, some notes about your job, and what the two of you like to do together. Give the journal to your grandchild the next time you see him or her. If you live far away, send it back and forth by mail approximately once a month. Depending on their financial situation, you may want to send postage for the child to send the journal back to you. Some children enjoy writing more than others, so don't get upset about a child who answers with only a line or two. Be brief with your entries and remember that some children don't know how to read or write cursive.

Some categories to consider:

- Funny jokes
- Interesting trivia
- Something you've learned from the Bible
- Intriguing quotes
- Challenging questions for the child to answer. Example: Why do you think Jonah disobeyed God? Why do you think people wouldn't listen to the message of Christ when he was staying right there in their town? Why do you think some students at school ignore God?

- Drawings
- Quizzes
- Lists such as ten places I'd like to go, twenty things I'm thankful for, ten favorite books I've read
- Prayer requests
- Books to read
- A story. You write the first paragraph, your grandchild writes the second, and so on.
- Invite your grandchild to share a joke, trivia, Bible verses, quotes, drawings, stories about school, and questions for you to answer.
- Not every entry needs to be about the Bible, but make sure that every entry aligns with the Bible.

Praying for Each Other

Grandparents have the opportunity to teach grandchildren to pray, and one way to do that is by looking up the prayers of Paul together to learn how he prayed. Here are three examples to get you started:

- **Ephesians 1:15–16** (NIV), "I heard about your faith in the Lord Jesus and your love for all God's people, I have not stopped giving thanks for you, remembering you in my prayers." *Grandchild version*: I am thankful you worked so hard learning that verse. I am thankful you helped your neighbor when she broke her ankle. I am thankful you started a Bible study with the students in your high school.
- **Philippians 1:9**, "that your love may abound more and more." *Grandchild version*: That you would be friendly to the new kid at school or church, that you may show love to your little brother and sister even though they annoy you, that you may be kind to Aunt Ima even though she buys you presents geared toward a toddler.

- **Colossians 1:9,** "asking that you may be filled with the knowledge of his will in all spiritual wisdom and understanding." *Grandchild version:* That you'll remember that verse about anger the next time the neighbor boy teases you. That you'll listen well to the lesson today. That you'll make the right decision about whether or not you should attend that party.

Most children learn to pray by listening to the adults around them, so we can pray with our grandchildren and model prayers that are filled with thankfulness, adoration, and requests on behalf of others. Ask your grandchild how you can pray for him or her and invite the grandchild to pray for you. Encouraging our grandchildren through prayer is a privilege. It is an opportunity to share requests, concerns, and things for which we are thankful. A grandchild who understands grandpa and grandma are praying for him or her is comforted as they go through the day, and knowing your grandchild is praying for you is also special.

Thirty Scriptures to Pray for Your Children and Grandchildren

Dear Father, I pray that (insert name in blank) . . .

Accept Advice

_____ will listen to constructive criticism and correction, and through it gain understanding (Proverbs 15:31–32).

Anger

_____ will be quick to listen and slow to speak, and slow to become angry (James 1:19).

Anxiety

_____ will cast all his/her anxieties and disappointments on you to experience your care for him/her (1 Peter 5:7).

Confidence

_____ will understand that the Lord is his/her helper and will always help him/her in every situation (Hebrews 13:6).

Compassionate

_____ will be kind, compassionate, and forgiving to others (Ephesians 4:32).

Contentment

_____ will learn to be content in every situation (Philippians 4:12).

Direction

_____ will acknowledge you in all his/her ways and you will direct his/her path (Proverbs 3:6).

Friendships

_____ will pursue righteousness, faith, love, and peace, and enjoy the companionship of those who love the Lord (2 Timothy 2:22).

Future Mate

_____ will find a spouse who loves Jesus and is in a growing relationship with Him (2 Corinthians 6:14).

Generosity

_____ will be generous and willing to share with others (1 Timothy 6:18).

Good Listener

_____ will guard his/her heart, for it is the wellspring of his/her life (Proverbs 4:23).

Hunger for God's Word

_____ will hunger and thirst for God's Word (Matthew 5:6).

Humility

_____ will do nothing out of selfish ambition, always considering others better than his/her self (Philippians 2:3).

Obedience to God

_____ will show his/her love for you by his/her obedience to you (John 14:15).

Obedience to Parents

_____ will learn to obey his/her parents (Ephesians 6:1).

Peace

_____ will not worry about anything, but pray about everything (Philippians 4:6).

Protection from the Enemy

_____ will be alert and watch out for the temptations of the enemy, standing firm in his/her faith (1 Peter 5:8–9).

Responsibility

_____ will learn to be responsible for his/her own actions and behavior (Galatians 6:5).

Salvation

_____ will believe that Jesus loves him/her and repent of his/her sins so he/she can enjoy eternal life (John 3:16).

Security

_____ will always remember that You will never leave or forsake him/her (Joshua 1:5).

Self-Control

_____ will live in this world with self-control, right conduct, and devotion to God (Titus 2:12).

Servant's Heart

_____ will develop a servant's heart, serving wholeheartedly, as unto the Lord and not men (Ephesians 6:7).

Speech

_____ will keep his/her tongue from evil and his/her tongue from lying (Psalm 34:13).

Spiritual Growth

_____ will be rooted and built up in his/her faith, growing strong in the truth as he/she is taught (Colossians 2:7–8).

Success

_____ will submit to you the desires of his/her heart and trust you with all his/her plans (Psalm 20:4).

Thanks

_____ will learn to give thanks in everything, no matter what happens (1 Thessalonians 5:18).

Timidity/Fear

_____ will not have a spirit of fear and timidity, but the spirit of power, love, and self-discipline (2 Timothy 1:7).

Trust the Lord

_____ will trust You with all his/her heart and not depend on his/her own understanding (Proverbs 3:5).

Wisdom

When _____ needs wisdom, he/she will turn to the Bible
and seek godly counsel from others (Psalm 19:7–14).

Work Ethic

_____ will work hard/cheerfully in all he/she does, pleasing the Lord, not men (Colossians 3:23).

Intentional Meals

Long-Distance Dinners

When your children and grandchildren live far away, meals together don't happen regularly. Use the following ideas to host your family and eat "together" even though you are not in the same room.

- Plan to make the same recipe for lunch or dinner on the same night. Grocery delivery services such as InstaCart or Amazon Fresh allow you to send them the fresh groceries needed to prepare the meal, if your budget allows. Video chat via FaceTime, Skype, or Facebook Messenger during the meal. Pray together, and enjoy chatting around the table as you would if you were together!
- Pizza delivery: Order pizza for your grandchildren and have it sent to their house as a surprise. (Coordinate this

with parents first.) Many delivery services offer desserts and beverages. What a treat for the entire family!

Bake a Simple Recipe Two Different Ways

Don't let food allergies, sensitivities, and dietary preferences hold you back from sharing meaningful moments baking and cooking with your grandchildren. Simple recipes can quickly become family classics because they are easy to prepare, delicious, and can be prepared for multiple occasions.

Before you begin baking, take into consideration the ages and ability levels of your grandchildren. Consider the following:

- Clear enough counter space for you and them to work without constraint.

- Keep your kitchen a safe space. Remind children not to touch hot surfaces, climb on counters or chairs to reach items up high, or operate appliances they are not familiar with.

- Messes and spills are going to happen. Recognize that in advance and do not shame your grandchild if accidents occur.

- Glass bowls and expensive cookware are wonderful for your own use, but consider using plastic bowls and utensils if you are concerned about anything being broken by little hands.

The following pages show the same recipe made two different ways. The first recipe is a classic quick bread. It is made with vegetable oil, sugar, and white flour. While the pumpkin provides a valuable nutrition source, parents who are concerned about their child's sugar and refined flour intake or parents of children with gluten allergies will not prefer this option.

Classic Pumpkin Quick Bread

Mulvihill Family Tradition

1 15-oz. can of 100% pumpkin puree
1 cup vegetable oil
2¾ cups sugar
3 eggs
3½ cups unbleached flour
½ teaspoon baking powder
1 teaspoon baking soda
1 teaspoon ground cloves
1 teaspoon ground nutmeg
1 teaspoon allspice
1 teaspoon cinnamon
1 teaspoon salt

Cooking instructions:

1. Move oven rack to low position so that the tops of the pans will be in the center of the oven.

2. Preheat oven to 325 degrees. Generously grease two bread loaf pans; set aside.

3. Mix pumpkin, oil, sugar, and eggs in large bowl or mixer. Stir in remaining ingredients. Pour into pans.

4. Bake for 60 minutes at 325 degrees. Cool before serving.

5. Wrap tightly and store at room temperature for up to five days.

This second recipe is similar to the Classic Pumpkin Quick Bread but contains a few simple modifications and uses organic ingredients and whole wheat flour. The caloric, sugar, and fat content is reduced by substituting applesauce for the oil. Adding nuts and seeds (if your grandchild doesn't have a nut allergy) adds healthy fats, protein, and vitamin E, along with calcium and magnesium.

Healthy Pumpkin Quick Bread

adapted by Jen Mulvihill

1 15-oz. can	of organic 100% pure pumpkin
¾ cup	unsweetened organic applesauce
2 cups	organic cane sugar
3	eggs
3 cups	organic whole wheat flour
½ teaspoon	baking powder
1 teaspoon	baking soda
1 teaspoon	ground cloves
1 teaspoon	ground nutmeg
1 teaspoon	allspice
1 teaspoon	cinnamon
1 teaspoon	salt

Optional: Add favorite nuts or seeds, cranberries, raisins, or mini chocolate chips for an indulgent treat!

Cooking instructions:

1. Move oven rack to low position so that the tops of the pans will be in the center of the oven.

2. Preheat oven to 325 degrees. Generously grease two bread loaf pans; set aside.

3. Mix pumpkin, applesauce, sugar, and eggs in large bowl or mixer. Stir in remaining ingredients. Pour into two pans.

4. Bake for 60 minutes at 325 degrees. Cool before serving.

5. Wrap tightly and store at room temperature for up to five days.

Checklist for Successful Mealtimes with Small Children

Many grandparents mention that they don't like serving meals to their grandchildren because of the chaos, mess, and work involved.

Mealtimes with small children can be a lot of work, especially when many family units are gathered at one time. We get it, but don't let this deter you from engaging in meaningful family meals. Instead, plan ahead for a successful mealtime experience for your family that involves the little ones and meets their needs.

- Manage expectations. Prepare yourself mentally for accidents, spills, and short attention spans.
- Gather necessary tools for a successful meal. Check out resale shops such as Once Upon a Child, garage sales, and Craigslist for inexpensive baby and toddler gear.
  - » High chair or booster seats
  - » Bibs
  - » Sippy cups
  - » Plastic/nonbreakable plates, cups, and bowls
  - » Extra spoons. Most little ones use spoons before they use forks. Have extras in case they are dropped or get dirty.
- Plan ahead for spills and messes. Serve your meal in a non-carpeted area. Have paper towels or baby wipes on hand.
- Unless a spill is going to cause a stain (such as grape juice on white carpet), do not interrupt mealtime to clean up. Save cleanup until after everyone has finished.
- Keep the menu child friendly. While this does not mean you need to serve chicken nuggets or mac and cheese, it does mean you should ask your adult children what foods your grandchildren like to eat and do your best to accommodate.
- Know your grandchild's dietary restrictions. Gluten free? Dairy free? Peanut allergies? Organic preferences? Keep everyone's needs in mind when planning meals. A simple addition can make meals more enjoyable for everyone.
- Don't forget the babies! Have simple first finger foods on hand, such as bananas, raisins, cheese, or yogurt melts.

- Remember the needs of your adult children. Serve food in a manner that will allow them to eat comfortably and engage in conversation, and not constantly be dishing up or cleaning up after their little ones. Consider placing all the food dishes on the table and passing them rather than having a buffet-style meal.

- Praise your grandchildren when you see them doing well. Great table manners, sitting up straight, saying please and thank you, using a napkin, asking before helping themselves to seconds, and politely declining foods they don't like should all be praised! Praise what is good, and do not draw attention to behaviors or skills that are lacking.

- Encourage grandchildren to try new foods, but don't force them. Similarly, do not scold children for not eating what's on their plate or scrutinize how much they have eaten. Allow their parents to monitor their food intake unless you are specifically asked for your advice.

- Keep the atmosphere positive with a "No biggie" attitude no matter the challenge. Spills? No biggie! Messes? No biggie! Not their favorite food? No biggie!

Practice Mealtime Manners with a Tea Party

While it is something many of us take for granted, the concept of table manners has largely become a lost art for the younger generations. Teaching table etiquette in a fun, informal way can become a meaningful way to connect with your grandchildren and make future mealtimes more smooth.

Invite your grandchildren to your home for a special high tea celebration. It can be something as simple as celebrating the day of the week—there is always an occasion! In advance, prepare a simple menu of desserts or snacks your grandchildren enjoy. When your grandchildren arrive, invite them to help you set the table to prepare for your celebration. Use this opportunity to teach the placement of dishes, silverware, glasses, and napkins. You can use anything from paper plates and napkins to fine china and cloth napkins. The activity can be as simple or as fancy as you make it, depending on your own preferences. Once the table is set, invite them to be seated. As you serve your celebration treats and eat them, teach the following very basic simple mealtime manners:

- The importance of washing their hands before coming to the table.
- The why and how of placing their napkin in their lap and setting it next to their plate when finished eating.
- Understanding when to use a spoon, fork, or knife.
- Where to place their knife when not using it.
- Show how putting elbows on the table can block conversation or even rock the table.
- Demonstrate in a lighthearted manner how to chew with their mouth closed and speak without a mouth full of food.
- Include a fun mealtime activity such as a question-and-answer game or Would You Rather? Example: Would you rather eat a cookie or a cupcake?

Do: Keep the tone positive and celebratory, even if they don't immediately demonstrate the manners you just taught.

Do: Serve food that is worthy of a celebration.

Do: Answer and ask questions to teach appropriate mealtime conversation.

Do: Have fun, laugh, and encourage your grandchild at the age and stage of learning they are in!

Learn about Missions by Enjoying an Ethnic Dinner

Enjoying an ethnic meal together is a great way to learn about other cultures and missions. Highlight a missionary you know and prepare a meal from the country where they are serving. Ask the missionary to send you recipes or invite them to share a meal with you and your grandchildren (when they are home from an assignment). Connecting the meal with actual people will personalize what you are doing. Here are some suggestions:

- Decorate using the flag and colors of the country you are highlighting.
- Look up John 3:16 in the language of the country. Check out Biblegateway.com.
- Search Amazon for cookies or crackers from the country you are focusing on. For example, Bis, a common Brazilian cookie, can be purchased on Amazon.
- Make place cards, a centerpiece, and other décor ahead of time. Include grandchildren in the activity, if they would enjoy helping.
- Ask an older grandchild to look up facts about the country to share with the family.
- If the missionary is not able to be with you, ask for facts about his or her work in the country and also how you can pray for them. As you pray, remember the missionary and the requests.
- Cook the meal together. Have your grandchildren decorate the table in honor of the country.
- Have fun with this idea. Perhaps you and your grandchildren could make a meal for the entire extended family!

Preparing Dinner with Bible Ingredients

Did you know that more than fifty foods are mentioned in the Bible? Make a meal with your grandchild that will be fun and increase knowledge about God's Word. Because there are so many foods mentioned, you could make a Bible-ingredient meal an annual tradition. To make the meal more meaningful, read the verses around the foods that you're using and discuss the context. Here are some suggested ingredients to make a complete meal:

- Calf (beef)—Luke 15:23
- Salt—Matthew 5:13
- Bread—John 6:48
- Cucumbers, onions, melon, garlic, leeks—Numbers 11:5
- Grapes, figs—Matthew 7:16
- Butter—Proverbs 30:33

For extra fun, make a cake or cookies from biblical ingredients. Linda has provided her recipe below. Her cake includes almonds, figs, and raisins, and she uses the King James Version. Consider looking up the verses with your grandchildren and having them figure out what ingredient you are to use.

Scripture Cake

½ cup   butter (Judges 5:25)
2 cups   sugar (Jeremiah 6:20)
2 T.   honey (1 Samuel 14:25)
6   eggs, separated (Jeremiah 17:11)
1½   cups flour (1 Kings 4:22)
2 tsp.   leaven (baking soda) (Amos 4:5)
Pinch   of salt (Leviticus 2:13)
Season to taste with spices (2 Chronicles 9:9)
Example: cinnamon (Exodus 30:23)
½ cup   milk (Judges 4:19)
1 cup   figs (Nahum 3:12)
½ cup   almonds (Numbers 17:8)
2 cups   raisins (I Samuel 30:12)

Cooking instructions:

1. Grease a 10″ tube pan. Preheat oven to 300 degrees.
2. Whip together the butter, sugar, and honey until light. Beat the six egg yolks and add to the mixture. (In a separate bowl, beat the egg whites until they form stiff peaks. Set aside.)
3. Mix together the flour, baking soda, salt, and any spices you desire to use. Combine with the creamed mixture, alternating with the milk.
4. Fold in the stiffly beaten egg whites. Fold in the figs, almonds, and raisins.
5. Pour mixture into the well-greased pan and bake for two hours. (Check after 90 minutes.)

Thanking Parents with a Dinner

Parents do a lot for children, and many children appreciate their parents. Young children bring bouquets of dandelions or draw pictures of hearts for their dad and mom. As children get older, they often want to do something more challenging but don't always have the expertise to carry out their plans. As grandparents, we can provide the help that is needed. Here is how:

- Plan a date with the parents. If the family lives close to you, you could invite the parents over for dinner and make the children's part be a surprise. If you live far away, plan a time that you're visiting. On a particularly busy day, let the parents know that you'll take care of the meal and then work with your grandchildren to plan a special dinner.

- Choose a verse together with your grandchildren for the theme of the meal. Remind them that the purpose of the meal is to show appreciation to their dad and mom.

- Have children write out the verse on a banner, chalkboard, poster board, or construction paper. As they work, discuss the meaning of the verse. Here are some options:
  » "Hear, my son, your father's instruction, and forsake not your mother's teaching" (Proverbs 1:8).
  » "Her children rise up and call her blessed; her husband also, and he praises her" (Proverbs 31:28).
  » "Train up a child in the way he should go; even when he is old he will not depart from it" (Proverbs 22:6).
  » "My son, keep your father's commandment, and forsake not your mother's teaching" (Proverbs 6:20).
  » "Honor your father and mother" (Ephesians 6:2).
- Make a meal plan and shopping list with your grand-children. Choose something simple, unless you truly have a chef among your grandchildren. Spaghetti is a good op-tion, as it is easy to prepare with little chance of failure.
- Purchase the needed ingredients.
- Prepare the meal.
- Set the table and include a creative centerpiece or place-mats. Children can use pictures of their parents or favorite possessions in their design. You could provide a large sheet of newsprint or a paper tablecloth. Give your grand-children crayons or markers so they can write random rea-sons they are thankful for their parents on the paper. Then use the masterpiece as the tablecloth.
- Choose a child to pray. He or she should thank the Lord for the food *and* for his or her parents!
- Serve the meal. Encourage the children to hold out their mom's and dad's chairs and to serve the honored guests first.
- Clear the table and wash and dry the dishes.
- Throughout the process, encourage the kids to tell their parents how much they appreciate them.

4

Teaching God's Word and Telling God's Work

Disciple a Grandchild Using a Good Book

Choose a Bible-based, Gospel-centered book that you can work through with your grandchild. If your grandchild lives close by, set up a recurring time to meet once a week, every two weeks, or once a month. If your grandchild lives far away, you can connect by video call using Zoom, FaceTime, or other video resources. Purchase two copies of a book; give one to your grandchild, and keep one for yourself. Read a chapter or portion and discuss it when you meet or talk on the phone. Some excellent books for grandchildren in grade school include:

- *Pilgrim's Progress* (children's version) by John Bunyan
- *How to Study Your Bible for Kids* by Kay Arthur
- *What Does the Bible Say About That? A Biblical Worldview Curriculum for Children* by Kevin Swanson
- *God's Names* by Sally Michael
- *The Lion, the Witch and the Wardrobe* by C.S. Lewis

Books for grandchildren who are teens include:

- *Know Why You Believe* by Paul Little
- *Essential Truths of the Christian Faith* by R. C. Sproul
- *Thoughts for Young Men* by J. C. Ryle
- *What Is the Gospel?* by Greg Gilbert
- *Don't Waste Your Life* by John Piper
- *Just Do Something* by Kevin DeYoung
- *The Holiness of God* by R. C. Sproul
- *Total Truth* by Nancy Pearcey
- *Money, Possessions, and Eternity* by Randy Alcorn
- *Church History Made Easy* by Timothy Paul Jones

Wonderful Things in God's Word

Psalm 119:18 states, "Open my eyes that I may see the wonderful things in your law." Have a discussion with your grandchildren about the wonderful things you have read in God's Word. Share with your grandchild some glorious truths you've read or passages God has used to encourage you. Invite your grandchild to share a WT, or wonderful thing, that has jumped out as he or she has read the Bible. If a grandchild can't think of anything, open the Bible and turn to a passage such as "Blessed are the peacemakers" (Matthew 5:9) or "God is our refuge and strength, a very present help in trouble" (Psalm 46:1).

Utilize Your Skills by Teaching What You Know

We informally interviewed individuals about their favorite memories with their grandparents, and overwhelmingly, the most common response was the time and conversations that occurred while spending time with their grandparents doing ordinary tasks. The over-the-top gifts and experiences were mentioned as highlights, but the most meaningful moments were shared working and being together.

Teach your grandchildren what you know and are passionate about. A shared skill or passion will open doors for repeated experiences together, establishing a deeper relationship, and will be something both of you look forward to doing together. Time spent together doing an activity you both enjoy breaks down barriers and gives the opportunity for conversation at a deeper level. You will have many opportunities to point your grandchild toward Christ as you talk with one another and learn more about your shared activity.

Take a moment to assess what skills you could share with your grandchildren. Here are some ideas:

- Art: painting, watercolors, pottery, drawing, photography
- Sewing, quilting, or knitting
- Music
- Cleaning and household maintenance
- Food: cooking, grilling, smoking
- Woodworking
- Sports
- Outdoors: fishing, hunting, camping
- Games: cards, chess, cribbage
- Morse code, ham radio
- Writing
- Gardening, raising animals

In each season of your grandchild's life, consider the following approaches to teaching:

- Little years: Introduction to materials and concepts, aim for positive experiences, plan for shorter attention spans and less coordination.

- Elementary: Teach basic techniques and concepts, attempt simple projects together, celebrate success, gift your special creations for them to enjoy.
- Teen years and adult: Teach more advanced techniques and projects, set aside time to work alongside one another or create together. Spend time in quantity due to greater attention spans and concentration.

Participate in Education

Whether your grandchildren are in public school, private school, or homeschool, in preschool or working toward their PhD, they are spending a great deal of time in educational settings. Volunteering your time in their area of study will allow you to speak into their lives as they are learning.

- Offer to tutor a specific subject after school.
- Read to your grandchild's elementary school classroom.
- Teach a subject for homeschool or co-op.
- Volunteer as a lunch or hall supervisor.
- Offer to help with carpooling.
- Help with school fundraising or PTA.
- Take a grandchild out for breakfast or donuts before school. Eat lunch with them at school.
- Start a Good News Club at your grandchild's school.
- Visit your grandchild at their college campus. Take them out to dinner or offer to take them to the store to stock up on food.
- If an adult grandchild is studying for an advanced degree, ask what they are studying.

Being a Good Friend

Children enjoy friendships but need help choosing good friends and learning how to develop relationships. Friendships are a gift from God, can give a child confidence, and keep children on the right path. A friendship with the wrong person can encourage a child or teen to make wrong choices, and sometimes those choices affect them for the rest of their lives. It is not uncommon for children to be mean to each other or bully one another. Girls can bounce from one friend to another, declaring someone is their best friend one day, but expressing hatred toward that person the next day. Boys can be cruel as well, often engaging in physical confrontations. As grandparents, we can encourage our grandchildren to put Christ in the center of their friendships and teach them the qualities of a gracious and godly friend. Here are some suggestions to speak into your grandchild's friendships:

- Encourage your grandchildren to choose friends wisely. Take an interest in their friends. If they live near you, get to know their friends by name.
- Tell short, interesting stories of your own friendships from childhood. If you are still close to any childhood friends, introduce them to your grandchild and together share stories of your adventures. Show your grandchild pictures of you and your friends when you were your grandchild's age.
- Invite your grandchild and his or her friend out to dinner, a ballgame, a concert, or to come stay at your house and visit for several days. You will need parental permission and a written medical note in case of emergency.
- Study the Bible together by reading and discussing verses that provide guidelines for friendship.

A friend puts the other person first. Read Philippians 2:4 together: "Let each of you look not only to his own interests, but also to the interests of others." Remind your grandchild that in our relationships we are to emulate Christ, who selflessly loves others. Take your grandchild along when you take soup to the neighbor who is laid up with a sprained ankle, or when you visit a friend in a nursing home. Let your grandchildren help you make cookies for the friend who subbed for you as leader of the Bible study last week. Let them see you mow the lawn for the widow, or cook a meal for the family who has the newborn. In all these ways, you are teaching them to put the other person first.

A friend is not sarcastic, quarrelsome, or deceitful. Proverbs 26:18–28 describes the way a fool talks. We are warned that a fool says hurtful things and then says it was only a joke (v. 19), is quarrelsome, gossips (vv. 20–21), and lies (vv. 24–28). Explain to your grandchild that these verses warn of the person who acts sweet and charming to your face, but is no longer kind when you walk away.

Friends do not brag to one another. Proverbs 16:18 reminds us that "Pride goes before destruction, and a haughty spirit before a fall." Explain to your grandchild that this doesn't mean they can't share good moments, but it does mean they shouldn't have an attitude of pride.

A friend is not argumentative. Read Proverbs 20:3: "It is an honor for a man to keep aloof from strife, but every fool will be quarreling." Explain to your grandchild that no one wants to be around someone who starts an argument about every little thing. Encourage your grandchild to be a peacemaker, to listen kindly to what the other person is saying, and when she does disagree, to do it respectfully.

A friend is loyal. Proverbs 17:17 states, "A friend loves at all times, and a brother is born for adversity." Explain to your grandchild that loyalty is not saying someone is your best friend one day and then saying you don't like the friend the next day. A friend is kind and helpful and is committed to the relationship every day.

A friend helps us grow in Christlike character. The writer of Proverbs states, "Iron sharpens iron, and one man sharpens another" (Proverbs 27:17). Good friends are profitable because God uses them to challenge each other to grow in Christlike maturity.

If your grandchild is older, challenge him or her to find additional verses that describe the qualities of friendship. (God's Word has a lot to say about life relationships.) Together, memorize John

15:13 about the greatest friend of all: "Greater love has no one than this, that someone lay down his life for his friends."

Teaching Biblical Manhood to Boys

We desire our boys to grow into strong, God-fearing men. One way to do that is to introduce them to biblical heroes. Boys want heroes and need good heroes. They need examples to follow. They need encouragement to choose heroes for the right reasons, such as courage or godliness, rather than fame or the number of social media followers. A recent study showed that children consider bravery the main quality of a hero. More than 35 percent said that their mom or dad was their hero, and nine percent said that their grandparents were their heroes. You can do the following things:

- Define the word *hero* and study a Bible character. A hero is a person who is respected for doing something courageous, notable, selfless, or brave. Discuss what heroes their friends or classmates admire. Ask your grandchild if their friends' heroes fit the definition. Choose a heroic Bible character and study the character's life together; suggestions include Jesus, Ruth, Joseph, David, Esther, Daniel, Paul, or Timothy. Discuss whether or not the person's decisions were difficult ones. What circumstances helped or discouraged him/her from making the right decision? What would he have done in the same situation? Encourage your grandson to be a hero by living a life pleasing to the Lord.
- Read the book *Ten Boys Who Made a Difference* or *Ten Boys Who Changed the World* together and discuss each hero presented.
- Purchase the audio book *Thoughts for Young Men* by J. C. Ryle and listen to the book while you take a day trip or weekend getaway and discuss J. C. Ryle's advice for young men.

- Purchase birthday or Christmas presents that provide a
  vision for manhood for your grandson. Any gift that will
  help a young man learn to serve others, protect, provide,
  and lead are good gifts. We have given tools, hunting and
  fishing items, pocket knives, and books about biblical
  manhood (*God's Design* by Sally Michael is a great book
  for grade-school boys).

- Grandfathers, share your wisdom about becoming a godly
  man. What wisdom have you gained over your lifetime?
  What successes can you pass on? What struggles have you
  experienced that you want your grandson to avoid?

Go on a Virtual Tour of Israel

Build your grandchildren's trust in God's Word by showing them
that the places and events of the Bible are real. Some children won-
der if the places in the Bible are real or fictional. Locate pictures,
DVDs, and web cams of Israel (and other Bible lands) to help your
grandchildren understand the trustworthiness of God's Word.

- Talk to your grandchildren about the difference between
  the fictional Hundred Acre Wood, Shire of Middle Earth,
  and Hogwarts, and the reality of Bethlehem, Jerusalem, or
  the Sea of Galilee.

- Do a Google search for the names of sites and cities such
  as Jericho, Cana, the Mount of Olives, or the Garden
  Tomb. Look at restaurant recommendations or houses for
  sale. These types of websites cement in your grandkids'
  minds that these places are real.

- Explore Google Maps. For instance, look up Capernaum.
  You can see where it is in relation to the Sea of Galilee,
  and you can also see the synagogue ruins. The ruins are
  not exactly where Jesus spoke, but these are ruins of a
  later synagogue on the same spot. The floor of the original

synagogue is several feet underground. They have excavated so people can see the foundation of the original. You can virtually walk down the streets of Jerusalem, Tel Aviv, or Bethlehem. Warning! This is fun, and you might find yourself spending a lot of time exploring.

- Go on YouTube and take a virtual tour of places mentioned in the Bible.

- If you've been to Israel, show your pictures, videos, or artifacts to your grandchildren.

- As you research pictures and videos, ask: Is that how you pictured the place looking? What do you think is different about this scene today from what it was in Bible times? How does seeing the picture of the land help you understand what we read, and support your belief that the Bible is true?

- Would you be able to visit Israel with an older grandchild? It's expensive, but worth it because of the spiritual impact and memories made together.

Take Notes in Church

Research has shown that taking notes helps us learn more and remember what we learn longer. Note-taking also keeps us from being distracted. Taking notes on a sermon helps us remember what we've learned about God's Word. The best way to encourage grandchildren to take notes is to do so ourselves.

- Are your grandchildren too young to write? Draw a picture of the pastor's main sermon points. Is he talking about the Red Sea? Draw a picture. Is he talking about God's love? Draw a heart.

- Does your church hand out note pages with blanks or numbers that correspond with what's being written on a screen? Fill in your own sheet and allow your grandchild to copy.

- Do your older grandchildren like notebooks? Buy them a church notebook and let them keep a journal of notes. To get them started, you can write down specific things you want them to look for, such as five sentences the pastor said, three verses used, three songs we sang, or the number of times the pastor says the word "Jesus."
- Do you use a print Bible at church? Help your grandchild find the verses in their own Bible. If your grandchild doesn't own a Bible, purchase one for him or her. Depending on the circumstances, you might want to get the parents' permission.
- Do you discuss what you've learned after the service? You can encourage your grandchildren to write down any questions they have about what the pastor said.

Participate in the Great Backyard Bird Count

The Great Backyard Bird Count is a designated four days when people around the world count and identify birds in their own backyard, listing what they see and hear. Some participants do this for only fifteen minutes, while others participate for days. The purpose is to help ornithologists record data necessary to know which bird populations are growing and which are in danger of extinction. There are other benefits for a grandparent and grandchild to participating, such as:

- Stand in awe of God by recognizing the details and design of His creation. He created so many different birds. Read about them.
- Learn to identify birds by sight and sound. Listen to the birds and observe them. You need to be quiet to hear them. They are all around, but we don't always see them.
- Information about the Great Backyard Bird Count can be found at https://www.audubon.org/conservation/about-great-backyard-bird-count. Register on the site.

- Purchase a bird identification book or app if you aren't familiar with your local birds.

- Before observing birds, read the biblical creation account with your grandchildren either in person or via video or FaceTime.

- Make the day special. Snack on sunflower seeds and apple slices, foods a bird might enjoy. As you are watching for birds, hang a bird feeder in the yard or make a birdhouse.

- Challenge your grandchild to find five verses about birds in the Bible. You do the same. Verses about birds:

  » "And God said, "Let the waters swarm with swarms of living creatures, and let birds fly above the earth across the expanse of the heavens" (Genesis 1:20).

  » "Who teaches us more than the beasts of the earth and makes us wiser than the birds of the heavens?" (Job 35:11).

  » "I know all the birds of the hills, and all that moves in the field is mine" (Psalm 50:11).

  » "Beasts and all livestock, creeping things and flying birds!" (Psalm 148:10).

  » "And as he sowed, some seed fell along the path, and the birds came and devoured it" (Mark 4:4).

  » "Then he sent forth a dove from him, to see if the waters had subsided from the face of the ground" (Genesis 8:8).

  » "In the evening quail came up and covered the camp, and in the morning dew lay around the camp" (Exodus 16:13).

  » "Who provides for the raven its prey, when its young ones cry to God for help, and wander about for lack of food?" (Job 38:41).

  » "Is it at your command that the eagle mounts up and makes his nest on high?" (Job 39:27).

» "Even the sparrow finds a home, and the swallow a nest for herself, where she may lay her young, at your altars, O Lord of hosts, my King and my God" (Psalm 84:3).

Biblical Worldview Detector

Train your grandchildren to detect erroneous messages from culture, school curricula, or media by examining the ideas and comparing them to the Bible. Colossians 2:7–8 warns us not to be captured by human philosophy or ideas, and we want to equip our grandchildren to recognize and reject ideas that don't align with God's Word. Here are two ideas to get you started:

- Listen to the song *Let It Go* from the Disney movie Frozen. Ask your grandchild to listen carefully for anything that may not align with the Bible. You can point out the line, "No right, no wrong, no rules for me. Let it go." Ask what this idea teaches. Ask who determines right and wrong.
- Watch the introduction to *Cosmos* by Carl Sagan. It can be found by a Google search or on YouTube. Carl begins by saying, "The Cosmos is all that is, or ever was, or ever will be." At about the three-minute mark he states, "We are made of star stuff." Discuss how an evolutionary view of creation is at odds with Genesis 1.

Tell about Past Generations

Grandparents are the keepers of a family's traditions, stories, and heritage. Teaching grandchildren about prior generations can teach essential lessons about God, life, family, and our eternal purpose. The following are ideas for sharing your faith and family heritage:

- Share your parents', grandparents', and great-grandparents' stories. Tell of their accomplishments, failures, funny memories, overcoming of adversity, and the way the world has changed since those beloved family members were living. What were your personal interactions with them? Most important, share their faith and godly or ungodly character. What was their faith background? Did they live their faith? When and where did they live and die? What can we learn from their life? What is worth imitating or doing differently?

- Show your children and grandchildren items in your home that have been passed down from prior generations. Consider writing down who items are from and their significance so these stories can continue to be told for many generations.

- Use photos to show grandchildren photos of their ancestors. Point out family resemblances and traits.

- Explore ancestry.com to learn about your family history.

- Cook recipes that are family traditions from your childhood. Give copies of these recipes to your children and grandchildren.

- Take your grandchildren on a historical tour of the cities where past generations lived. Plan a road trip and drive to the family homestead, visit grave sites, and explore the landscape where your relatives worshiped, lived, and died. If these locations are far away, consider using Google Maps.

Share Your Faith Story

A famous hymn states, "This is my story, this is my song, praising my Savior all the day long."[1] Our story isn't the point, it's the pointer. God wants to use our life history and testimony to tell about His character and nature (Psalm 78:4–5). Everyone has a story to tell, and My Hope 2 U is a ministry that helps you share your story. You begin by visiting the website mh2u.org; sign up and you will be provided a journal to help you write your story. Then you upload your story and photos onto the interactive website. Choose from the online database of reasons why Christianity is true, or write your own reasons. You will receive a full-color, fifty-two-page printed book. You can order as many copies as you would like of the same version, or duplicate and personalize for each person you would like to share your story with.

5

Reading and Memorizing the Bible

Check Out Unusual Verses

Many phrases have been attributed to the Bible when, in actuality, they were written by Shakespeare or Ben Franklin. And many times we hear someone use a phrase and don't know they're quoting Scripture. The following activity can be entertaining, but at the same time it teaches us to research our sources and become more familiar with God's Word.

When your grandchildren are visiting, or you're visiting them, you could have fun quizzing each other around the dinner table. If you live far away, you could share one phrase a day. Challenge your grandchildren to come up with their own phrases to challenge you. Can you stump them? Can they stump you? Choose some sayings that do not sound as if they're from the Bible even though they are. Choose others that aren't from the Bible but sound as if they are. You will find a list of such phrases below, but don't stop with these. Research further and find more.

- *Like mother, like daughter.* Ezekiel 16:44: "Behold, everyone who uses proverbs will use this proverb about you: 'Like mother, like daughter.'"
- God *helps those who help themselves.* This phrase originated in ancient Greece and was later attributed to Ben Franklin. Although a lot of people think this is Scripture, this is the exact opposite of what Scripture teaches. We are helpless without God.
- *Of making many books there is no end, and much study is a weariness of the flesh.* The passage is found in Ecclesiastes 12:12.
- *The suburbs shall shake at the sound of the cry of thy pilots.* You can find this verse in Ezekiel 27:28 (KJV). The word *suburbs* referred to cities, as it does now, and the *pilots* are captains of ships.
- *Necessity is the mother of invention.* This is often attributed to Plato, as it appears in a translation of his *Republic.*
- *The skin of my teeth.* It's in Job 19:20: "My bones stick to my skin and to my flesh, and I have escaped by the skin of my teeth."
- *No city or house divided against itself will stand.* We often think of this phrase in relationship to the Civil War, but it was said by Christ in Matthew 12:25: "Knowing their thoughts, he said to them, 'Every kingdom divided against itself is laid waste, and no city or house divided against itself will stand.'"
- *Give a man a fish and you feed him for a day; teach a man to fish and you feed him for a lifetime.* This anonymous proverb is not from the Bible.
- *Do not throw your pearls before pigs.* It's found in Matthew 7:6: "Do not give dogs what is holy, and do not throw your pearls before pigs, lest they trample them underfoot and turn to attack you."

- *A drop from a bucket.* This passage is found in Isaiah 40:15: "Behold, the nations are like a drop from a bucket, and are accounted as the dust on the scales; behold, he takes up the coastlands like fine dust."
- *A rose by any other name would smell as sweet.* This is from Shakespeare's *Romeo and Juliet.*
- *Do not go where the path may lead, go instead where there is no path and leave a trail.* Ralph Waldo Emerson is commonly credited with writing this phrase, which is not in the Bible.
- *I am a laughingstock to my friends.* Most children feel this way at one time or another. Job felt this way too, which is why he said, "I am a laughingstock to my friends; I, who called to God and he answered me, a just and blameless man, am a laughingstock" (Job 12:4).
- *There is more power in a mother's hand than in a king's scepter.* Not found in the Bible, but said by Billy Sunday.

Make Magnets to Memorize a Verse

Colossians 3:16 states, "Let the word of Christ dwell in you richly, teaching and admonishing one another in all wisdom, singing psalms and hymns and spiritual songs, with thankfulness in your hearts to God." For the word of Christ to dwell (live) in us, we must know that Word, and to know the Word, it helps to memorize the Word.

Memorization takes work, but there are ways to make it fun. An established way to memorize, used by thousands of children's ministry leaders and parents over the years, is to write out the verse and then erase the words one by one and after each word is eliminated, repeat the verse again. Another common method is to put each word on a separate piece of paper, shuffle the words, and then once again put them in order. Using magnets is a variation of that last activity, but can also be a method for the entire family to learn the verse together since magnets will stick to most refrigerator surfaces and be in plain sight.

- Make your magnets by purchasing magnetic tape from a craft store or order online.
- Choose a verse for both you and your grandchild to learn the next time he or she comes to visit.
- Print out the verse and cut it up so that each word is on a separate piece of paper. Back each word with the magnet tape.
- Mix up the words and have children put them in order. For younger children, start with just four or five words.
- Put the words in the correct order. Read the verse with your grandchild. Allow your grandchild to remove one word at a time. After each word is eliminated, repeat the verse again. Remove another word. Repeat until there aren't any words remaining and you and your grandchild can quickly say the entire verse.
- Allow children to use the refrigerator to practice.
- Make a set of the magnets for each grandchild. You could then have contests to see who completes the verse first.
- Make a to-go set. Magnets will stick to most cookie sheets, so children can practice putting the verse together in the yard or car.
- You could also use the magnets to learn other Bible facts. Write a list of Bible events on the magnets. Have your grandchildren put them in chronological order. Make a set of the books of the Bible and practice putting all sixty-six books in order.

Use Objects to Memorize

Children use different methods for memorizing verses. Using objects to learn a verse is a great method for visual and/or active learners, but works for other types of learners as well. Many children learn better when they're moving around. Associating an object with a word in a verse can enhance learning. Here is an example:

- Choose a verse such as Psalm 119:48: "I will lift up my hands toward your commandments, which I love, and I will meditate on your statutes."
- Set up stations around the house that each represent a different word or phrase.
- Use a song book or piano sheet music to illustrate the word Psalm. Attach a piece of paper to the cover of the songbook or sheet music that reads 119:48.
- Put gloves or mittens on a table to signify hands. Stop and lift them up, then put them down again because you'll need them for the next time around.
- Display an instruction book of some kind to represent commandments.
- Put a heart on a shelf for love.
- Place a Bible on a chair signifying meditating.
- Do you have a doll or china figure of a person? The Psalm says statute, not statue, but sometimes doing something silly or not quite right will help a grandchild remember. Explain the difference to your grandchild.
- Walk around the house from station to station saying the verse. Do this several times until both you and your grandchild are able to repeat the verse. You might be surprised how quickly you can memorize the entire verse.

Bible Character Biography

The Bible character biography is an opportunity to study men and women of the Bible and learn from them. Paul tells the Corinthians, "These things happened [events and people in history] to them as an example, but they were written down for our instruction" (1 Corinthians 10:11). Utilize character biographies as an example, to learn from their failures and successes. You will find that children may not know many details about some Bible characters, so it will be valuable to introduce them to their actual life story. They may know a lot about a few favorites, but little about people such as Ehud, Dinah, Demas, Heman, or Absalom. Choose a person of the month to study with your grandchild. Think about these people as real men and women (because they are), and in doing so, help your grandchildren to grow in their knowledge and understanding of God's Word. What to do:

- Choose a Bible character to study each month. You can choose some months and ask your grandchild to choose other months.

- Learn as much as you can about the person. Ask questions: Where did they live? What family members did they have? What was their occupation? What was the meaning of their name? When did they live? Where do they fit into the timeline of the Bible? What is the context of their story? (What is happening around them?) What is their relationship with God? How did this person fit into God's plan of salvation? What are the events of their life recorded in Scripture? Why was their story told?

- Memorize a verse about the person or written by the person.

- Search the web for pictures of towns where the person visited. For instance, there is a statue of Paul in Malta. Search the web for videos that explain the life of the person you are studying.

- Start with individuals who have several chapters written about them, such as Abraham, Joseph, David, or Paul. Then choose some who aren't mentioned as frequently, such as Rahab, Zacchaeus, or Philemon.

- Encourage your grandchild to remember what they've learned by drawing a picture about the person; make a storyboard that includes several pictures of the person's life, write a newspaper article about the character, role play an event in the character's life, retell the character's story, or write a journal from the person's point of view.
- Create a three-ring binder to save each Bible Character Biography. Encourage your grandchild to make a cover for it, such as "Aiden's Bible Study Book."

Memorize the Books of the Bible

Memorizing the Bible is never a waste of time. There are many reasons to memorize Scripture. The Psalmist provides one when he states, "How can a young man keep his way pure? By guarding it according to your word" (Psalm 119:9). We can encourage grandchildren to memorize Scripture, as it will help them live a life that is pure and holy. We can also encourage grandchildren to memorize the books of the Bible to know their way around God's Word. Here are some ideas to help your grandchildren memorize the books in order:

- Show your grandchild the table of contents in the Bible and explain that there are sixty-six smaller books within the bigger book.
- Explain that it's good to memorize the names of the books, in order, because it allows us to easily find a verse and to learn the chronology of the Bible.
- Explain the two testaments. Ask your grandchild to look up the pages that signify the break between the Old and New. Point out the difference in size.
- Explain that God inspired the words of the entire Bible by using different people to write down what He wanted them to write. Use biblical terminology that God inspired the words of the Bible.

- Explain chapters and verses. Chapters and verses help us find the places we're looking for in Scripture. The chapter and verse divisions are not inspired.

- A great way to memorize the books of the Bible is by singing the names of the books together. Download two songs to your phone or tablet: *Old Testament Hop* by Great Worship Songs Kids Praise Band and *The Only Way (The New Testament Song)* by Seeds Family Worship.

- If you don't know the books of the Bible, learn them with your grandchild. Have a race to see who can say them the fastest!

- Work together to be able to say the books quickly and with confidence. Periodically review the books so your grandchildren retain the names and order. Make it fun for them and for you!

Summarize the Books of the Bible

Work with your grandchild to learn the subject of each book of the Bible.

- You will need sixty-six 3x5 cards. Write the name of each book of the Bible on an individual card.

- Summarize each book of the Bible with your grandchildren, but don't do all the talking! Allow them to share their knowledge with you. What happened in the book of Genesis? What happened in Luke?

- Visit The Bible Project channel on YouTube and watch the video for each book of the Bible that you are summarizing. They also have a website, https://thebibleproject.com.

- Come up with one word or a short phrase that describes each book. Sometimes the title describes the meaning. For example, Genesis—beginnings; Exodus—the way out;

Psalms—songs of worship; Lamentations—songs of sadness; and Proverbs—God's wisdom for life.

Discuss the Sermon

Whether you have the privilege of attending the same church as your grandchildren or you live far away, make a habit of talking or texting about what you learned at church. The weekly discussion doesn't need to be long, but it can be a means of accountability to attend church and pay attention to the message as well as an opportunity to help a grandchild understand and apply God's Word.

- You will need paper and pen to write down questions and key points during the message.
- Ask key questions about the day's message in person, by phone, or by text.
- If your grandchildren have had a lesson on a subject you're unfamiliar with, ask your grandchild to tell you about three things he or she learned. Then in return, share three things you learned from the message at your church.

Study the Bible Together

A regular Bible study with your grandchild is a great way to learn together and to encourage a grandchild to develop the habit of spending time in God's Word. Show your grandchild how to read and study the Bible by learning how to observe context, interpret correctly, and apply what is learned to life. You can set up the Bible study in several ways. Choose a plan that works for your family.

- Choose a book of the Bible, Bible character, or topic to study. You could get some suggestions from your grandchild and then make the final choice. Make a plan to read through the book or topic based on the length of time the study will last.

- Explain to your grandchildren what you'll research in each passage: What is happening in this Scripture? What is the central theme of the passage? What is the application for life? What is being taught about God? Humanity? Jesus? What's your favorite verse from the passage?
- Read and discuss a book of the Bible or go through a devotional together. Consider utilizing Kids Bible Reading Plan for Genesis or Matthew, which will make Bible reading short, simple, and systematic. You can also utilize *How to Study Your Bible for Kids* by Kay Arthur, which is a systematic study of the book of Titus. For teens you could utilize *How to Study Your Bible* by John MacArthur.
- *Exploring the Bible* by David Murray is a wonderful resource. Purchase two copies of the book, one for you and one for your grandchild. If your grandchild lives close, meet regularly to work through the book. If your grandchild lives at a distance, schedule a video chat or phone call to discuss.
- If your grandchild is staying with you for a specific amount of time, concentrate on a short book of the Bible, such as Esther or Nehemiah, or a specific topic like the character of God or the fruit of the Spirit.
- Participate with grandchildren on something they are doing for church or school. Are your grandchildren memorizing verses for church? Why not memorize with them? Are they doing a Bible study? Why not do one too? Is your grandchild in a Bible study in middle or high school youth group? Invite your grandchild over and study the lessons together, which will help your grandchild stay motivated, and you both will learn from the study.
- For older grandchildren, you could purchase a journal so they can write what they are learning. Have them write their key verse from the passage along with other things they've learned.

- As you study the Bible with your grandchildren, continually point to the Gospel, the importance of knowing Christ as your Savior, and applying the Gospel to life.

Take Photos to Illustrate a Verse

Taking pictures to illustrate a verse is a great learning experience. Not only does it help the child or teen remember the words, but also challenges them to think about the meaning. Lots of children enjoy taking pictures. Many grandchildren have phones with camera capability or actual cameras. Take advantage of their interest, have fun, and learn more about God's Word.

Choose a verse with your grandchild that you can illustrate with pictures. Choose a verse that lends itself to pictures, not one that's abstract, such as genealogy. Look for a verse with good imagery. If you live far from your grandchild, you could both search for pictures to illustrate the verse and then compare. Some examples of good verses to illustrate with pictures.

- Psalm 148:3: "Praise him, sun and moon, praise him, all you shining stars!"
- Psalm 148:9–10: "Mountains and all hills, fruit trees and all cedars! Beasts and all livestock, creeping things and flying birds!"
- Proverbs 17:1: "Better is a dry morsel with quiet than a house full of feasting with strife."
- Proverbs 22:29: "Do you see a man skillful in his work? He will stand before kings; he will not stand before obscure men."
- Song of Solomon 2:11–12: "For behold, the winter is past; the rain is over and gone. The flowers appear on the earth, the time of singing has come, and the voice of the turtledove is heard in our land."

Look for pictures that represent the words in the Bible verse. If you can't find a picture, you may find the word itself. For example, you might not come up with a word that represents forever, but you may find the word "forever." You might not find a picture that represents the biblical David, but you can find the word *David*. When you are done taking pictures, put the pictures in order and design a display, either on poster board or digitally. Besides illustrating a verse, you can illustrate other concepts, such as the character of God, the days of creation, or the fruit of the Spirit.

6

Sharing the Gospel

EvangeCube

Sharing the truth of the Gospel is the most important thing you can ever do with your grandchildren. Utilize the following method to share the Gospel.

An EvangeCube resembles a Rubik's cube. When the cube is folded in various ways, the blocks of the cube form pictures that depict creation, sin, Jesus' death and resurrection, and forgiveness of sins. The EvangeCube is an effective, hands-on tool that will bring the Gospel to life for grandchildren of all ages. An Evange-Cube can be purchased by searching online. Video demonstrations are available on the web that show how to utilize the cube.

Wordless Book

The Wordless Book was first used by Charles Spurgeon in 1866 and is a tool utilized all over the world to explain the plan of salvation to children using colors. A wordless book is available for a couple of dollars from many online ministries. You can also create or use a bracelet with colored beads.

- Begin by showing your grandchild the wordless book. Tell him there are no words, but it is a very important story using only colors.
- Turn to the first page and use your own words to communicate how the colors of the book relate to the Gospel.
  - » Gold = Heaven. Heaven is a wonderful place where there is no sickness, sadness, or death. The most wonderful thing about heaven is that it is God's home. God loves us very much and wants us to be with him. But there is something that prevents us from being with God. Read Revelation 21:4.
  - » Black = Sin. Sin is rebellion against God's law and it is disobedience. It is doing what we want instead of what God wants. Every person has sinned. The punishment for sins is the wrath of God. God is perfect and just. He does not ignore or excuse sin. Read Romans 3:23 and 6:23.
  - » Red = The blood of Jesus. Jesus came to earth and lived a perfect life. Jesus paid the penalty of sin through His death on the cross and resurrection three days later. Read Romans 5:8 and John 3:16.
  - » White = Made clean. Jesus offers to take our sin and exchange it for His righteousness. A response is needed. We must believe in Jesus and repent of our sin. Read 1 John 1:9.
  - » Green = Growing in Christ. It is important for us to grow with Christ, and this happens as we pray, read the Bible, obey God, and become part of a community of believers.

Romans Road

Explain the path of salvation using verses from the book of Romans, sometimes referred to as the Romans Road to Salvation.

- The Problem: All have sinned, Romans 3:23.
- The Consequence: The wages of sin is death, Romans 6:23.
- The Solution: Christ died for us, Romans 5:8.
- The Response: Believe and repent, Romans 10:9.

Share the Gospel Using Five Fingers and Five Verses

Use the fingers of your hand to talk through five points of the Gospel and five Bible verses.

Begin by asking your grandchild if she knows for certain that when she dies she will go to heaven. Then ask if you may share with her how you know that you will go to heaven.

1. God loves me! (Point to your thumb.) John 3:16 says that "God so loved the world." This includes everyone. You, me, everyone, including those who have come before us, and everyone who will come after us.
2. I am a sinner. (Point to your pointer finger.) Romans 3:23 says, "All have sinned." The word *all* means everyone, including you and me. Romans 6:23 says the penalty (or wages) for our sins is death, or eternal punishment for sins. That is not good news. But, there is good news!
3. Jesus died for me. (Point to your middle finger.) That is good news! First Corinthians 15:3–4 tells us that Jesus died on the cross and was raised on the third day to pay the penalty for our sins. Jesus loves us a lot to die for us while we were still sinners.
4. If I believe . . . (Point to ring finger.) Ephesians 2:8–9 tells us that our path to everlasting life, living with God forever,

is only through faith. It is a free gift, not something we can earn. We are invited to believe in Jesus and repent of our sins.

5. I go to heaven. (Point to pinky.) John 3:16 says that "whoever believes in Him should not perish but have everlasting life." That means when we die, we live in heaven with God forever!

Is there any reason why you would not want to respond to Jesus by faith today? You can do it right now by praying this prayer: "Dear Jesus, I confess that I am a sinner. I believe that you died and rose again to pay the penalty for my sins. I ask you to forgive me of my sins and be the King of my life. I want to live for you. Thank you! I pray in Jesus' name, Amen."

Dirty Water Experiment

- Fill a clear glass or pitcher half full with water. Drop one to two drops of food coloring into the water to represent our sin.

- Put some bleach or bleach mixed with water in another similarly sized glass or pitcher.

- Pour the bleach water into the glass of dirty water and mix the two liquids well. Let the mixture sit for a minute and watch the food color disappear. Explain how this is symbolic of what God will do in our heart when we believe in Jesus and repent of our sin.

Challenge Children to Think about Their Faith

Many children are growing up in the church, hearing a lot of stories, seeing a lot of exciting videos, watching a lot of funny skits, and making a lot of glittery crafts often without learning about God's Word or understanding the difference Christ can make in their lives. None of these activities are bad in moderation, but they can be a problem if they take the place of true learning. Some children can repeat the message of the Gospel but haven't truly grasped what it means to be a sinner in need of a Savior.

Grandparents have the opportunity to challenge grandchildren to think. We need to look for ways to challenge their faith and help them think through why they believe what they believe. We need to pray for wisdom as we interact with these precious young lives and be willing to enter into tough discussions. Here are a few suggestions:

- Read and discuss some verses that include the word "think." Here is one example: "Brothers, do not be children in your thinking. Be infants in evil, but in your thinking be mature" (1 Corinthians 14:20).

- Ask age-appropriate hard questions. As you're driving in the car, taking a hike, or baking cookies, ask, "How would you explain why bad things happen in the world?" Or, "What difference does being a Christian make in your life?"

- Create a hypothetical moral dilemma and ask what is right or wrong in that situation. Make some of the solutions tough to figure out. "You are babysitting, and the mother tells you not to pray or say anything about the Bible in front of the children again. What would you do?" "You have the lead role in a school play and discover when reading the script that you will have to use the Lord's name in a disrespectful way. What would you do?" "If you are at a friend's house and your friend's mom shows a movie that you know your parents wouldn't want you to watch, what would you do?"

- Take your grandchild to a biblical worldview conference or seminar. *The Christian Worldview* radio program has wonderful weekly radio broadcasts; also consider Summit Ministries and Renewanation.

- Answer any of their questions. Tell your grandchildren that they are always welcome to ask you questions and share thoughts with you.

- Challenging children to think is not something we do one afternoon at the beach, but is an ongoing attitude and a lifelong commitment that encourages a grandchild to know as much as he or she can about God's Word to faithfully serve Christ for all of life.

Answer Hard Questions

Children like to ask questions because they are curious about the world and want answers. Our goal is to become an askable grandparent who takes questions seriously. If we brush aside their questions, even the silly ones, when they're little, they won't ask us the more serious ones later on. Grandparents often get asked a lot of *why* questions, and as grandchildren get older, their questions go deeper. Our well-thought-out, caring answers to tough questions can be life-changing for our grandchildren as they consider their future. We have the opportunity and responsibility to provide the best answers possible.

A good grandparent-grandchild relationship can generate trust. Many times grandchildren will come to a grandparent with their questions when they hesitate to go to parents or other adults. They know they can trust Grandpa or Grandma not to laugh or respond with shock or anger.

Grandchildren whose parents don't take them to church will notice that you love the Lord and attend church, which may generate several questions as they realize that your weekly routine is different from their family routine. Answer their questions honestly. Invite them to attend church with you, if it's okay with their parents and they live in your city.

Grandchildren may ask you hard questions about God and the Bible. Be willing to sit down with them and show them where the answers are in God's Word. If you don't know the answer, work with them to research the answer. If you're still not sure of the answer, ask your pastor or other church staff member for help. Some excellent resources that may prove helpful to you include *Keeping Your Kids on God's Side* by Natasha Crain, *Preparing Children for Marriage* by Josh Mulvihill, *How Do We Know the Bible Is True* by Ken Ham and Bodie Hodge, *Jesus Among Other Gods (Youth Edition)* by Ravi Zacharias, and the ANSWERS series by Answers in Genesis.

In the middle of an activity with a grandchild, allow for some quiet moments and one-on-one time, giving grandchildren the opportunity to get into good conversations with you. Back up parents with solid support. Be the one who is there to answer children's questions so that others can say of your grandchildren, "I am reminded of your sincere faith, a faith that dwelt first in your grandmother" (2 Timothy 1:5).

Teach Children to Make Right Choices

It is a great joy when a grandchild trusts Christ, and an even greater privilege to be part of the child's decision. Once a grandchild comes to faith, our work is not over. Our role is to encourage grandchildren to follow Christ and grow in spiritual maturity. We can equip our grandchildren to be obedient to God and discern between right and wrong. The following poem was written by Linda to help children learn to make the right choice and live in obedience to God. We need to give our grandchildren biblical tools to help them spiritually mature into godly men and women. This poem is a good first step and a helpful tool:

> Stop and walk away!
> Then take the time to pray.
> Do Dad and Mom say it's okay?
> What does the Bible have to say?

The poem is in a specific order.

1. Stop and walk away! Children need to be encouraged to get out of the situation if they aren't sure whether or not it's the right thing to do. First Timothy 6:11 encourages young people, "But as for you, O man of God, flee these things. Pursue righteousness, godliness, faith, love, steadfastness, gentleness." Paul instructs us to flee the situation, not calmly walk away!

2. Then take the time to pray. A child shouldn't remain in a tempting situation, thinking about whether it is right or wrong. He needs to leave and then talk it over with the Lord. Matthew 26:41 states, "Watch and pray that you may not enter into temptation. The spirit indeed is willing, but the flesh is weak."

3. Do Dad and Mom say it's okay? You could replace the words *mom* and *dad* with *my grandparents*, especially if your grandchildren are staying at your house. A child has removed herself or himself from the situation, prayed about it, and needs to discuss with dad or mom, even if it is after they get home from school or the park. Proverbs 1:8 reminds children, "Hear, my son, your father's instruction, and forsake not your mother's teaching."

4. What does the Bible have to say? We want to train children to learn God's Word so they can apply it to every life situation they will face. When children are younger, they will need a parent or grandparent to help them apply the Bible to life, but as they grow older they will learn to do this on their own. Psalm 119:9 states, "How can a young man keep his way pure? By guarding it according to your word."

Write a Psalm

Does your grandchild enjoy writing? Encourage him or her to express his or her love, thankfulness, and praise by writing a psalm. Explain that by writing a psalm, you are not pretending that it's from God's Word. *Psalm* is the Hebrew word for song, and your grandchild will be writing a song about God through poetry. Write a psalm together or on your own and then share with one another.

This project will help your grandchild think about his or her relationship with Christ.

- You will need a Bible and fancy paper. A child can write a psalm on a computer if that's desired or if you are working on the psalm together and need to send ideas back and forth.
- Explain the meaning of the word *psalm*. Psalms is a book in the Bible that contains a collection of individual songs or psalms. Followers of God have used the Psalms in worship, singing praises, and playing instruments such as harps, trumpets, and cymbals.
- Decide if you're going to write the psalm together or separately. This is a fun activity for grandparents too!
- Read a selection of verses from Psalm 119. Explain that each section of Psalm 119 is a poem that begins with a different letter of the Hebrew alphabet.
- Suggest that your grandchild write about the characteristics of God, ways God shows His love toward us, or the things for which he or she is thankful. Your grandchild could choose to write the poem like Psalm 119, with each line or section starting with a different letter of the alphabet.
- Decorate the finished psalm.
- Make psalm writing a yearly tradition, writing about a different topic each year. Keep a notebook or computer file of your and your grandchild's work.

7

Serving Together

Get Involved in Their Activities

Most children, whether age two or forty-two, are involved in some sort of activity. Whether it's a toddler music class, Awana club, chess club, marching band, sport, or adult Bible study, there are many opportunities to invest spiritually with your grandchildren on a regular basis. Consider serving as a volunteer at their classes and clubs when grandchildren are in their school years.

- Volunteer to take your grandchild to mommy-and-me-style toddler classes.
- Serve as a Sunday school teacher, Wednesday evening Awana leader, or junior/senior high youth volunteer in their church.
- Offer to coach your grandchild's sport team. If you are unable to coach, ask about other ways to get involved with their team. Bringing and serving snacks, keeping score, or cheering the team at games has value.

- Be active in their school! Serve as hall monitor, lunch supervisor, or volunteer in their classroom.

- Utilize Bible study groups such as Bible Study Fellowship. Bring your adult child and grandchild to BSF and study God's Word together.

- Grandmas, invest in your adult daughters or daughters-in-law along with your grandchildren at a local moms group such as MOPS (Mothers of Preschoolers).

Practical Service Opportunities

Once our grandchildren have trusted Christ as Savior, we want them to be excited about serving Him. Sometimes the best way to do that is by example. We can do that by inviting them to join us when we serve. Sometimes it takes extra effort and it might be easier to do it by ourselves, but including our grandchildren is always worth it. Ephesians 2:10 states, "We are his workmanship, created in Christ Jesus for good works, which God prepared beforehand, that we should walk in them." Serving together develops a special bond and encourages a grandchild to serve Christ throughout life. Pray for opportunities to serve with your grandchild.

Before you serve together, you need to discuss with your grandchildren whether or not they know the Lord. In order to *serve* their Savior, they need to *know* their Savior. Serving can come in many forms. Here are some ideas:

- Is your church having a workday? Invite your grandchildren to come and serve with you. Even very young children can help. Once I had two preschoolers work alongside me, going through a couple hundred crayons in the children's department. They separated the broken crayons and pulled off the torn paper. They were proud that they could serve on a workday, and did an excellent job at a task that needed to be done and that no adult wanted to do.

- Are you musical? Could your grandchildren sing with you? Or maybe you could accompany that budding violinist or trumpeter.
- Can you make a meal for a new mom or someone recovering from surgery? A grandchild could help you cook, then deliver the food with you.
- Do you help clean the church building? Grandchildren can help dust or vacuum. Is it your turn to be a greeter? Your grandchild could stand with you and open the door or hand out worship folders. Do you teach Sunday school? Your grandchild can help you set up. Do you prepare worship folders or pick up empty communion cups? Invite your grandchild to join you.
- Serve with an older grandchild in children's ministry. It is a joy to be together, and the ride home provides an opportunity to discuss the grandchild's questions about the situations you observe. Once in a while, grab a Frosty or ice cream, especially when children are extra noisy or active.
- If your grandchild lives far away, it may be difficult to find service activities. You may be able to plan a serving opportunity when he comes to visit. One way to serve together, when living a distance from each other, is to raise money for the same cause.

Ways to serve at church:

- Serve in the nursery together or prep crafts and make photocopies for children's ministry.
- Greet or usher, prepare and clean up after communion, serve food at funeral luncheons.
- Bring treats to the church staff during the week.
- Sing in the choir or play in the band.
- Visit shut-ins. Prepare and deliver meals to those who are ill or moms with new babies.

- Work outside pulling weeds, picking up trash, mowing the lawn.
- Prepare seasonal décor, such as putting up and taking down Christmas trees.
- Write letters of encouragement to church-supported missionaries.

Ways to serve at home:

- Sort through unused clothes and household items and donate them to a local nonprofit clothing ministry. Tackle a project you've been putting off, such as organizing closets or deep cleaning window blinds.
- Grow a vegetable garden with the intention of donating the food to a food bank. Maintain the yard at their home or yours together.
- Offer to cook dinner together or clean the house for your adult children, and run errands that will help your adult children.
- Put together a care package for older siblings or cousins who are in college or the military. Shop together for a gift for a family member. Throw a baby shower or wedding shower for a sibling, cousin, or aunt.
- Start a lending library at the end of your driveway and decide together what books should be in the library.

Ways to serve in the community:

- Prepare Blessing Bags that include toiletries for women's shelters or homeless ministries.
- Run or walk a 5K to raise money for a cause you both are passionate about.

- Volunteer to host a fundraiser for a family in need. Participate in community park or roadside clean-ups. Collect nonperishable food items for a local food bank.
- Make no-tie blankets for hospitals and shelters.
- Pack shoeboxes for Operation Christmas Child.
- Create birthday bags that include cake mix, hats, candles, and balloons for local food banks.
- Take care of pets at an animal shelter.
- Give blood together.

Ways to serve at a distance: Serve in the same way at the same time; for example, you and your grandchild both could be a greeter at church. Hold separate bake sales to raise money for the same ministry. Sponsor a Compassion Child together and take turns communicating with the child, or sponsor two children and discuss your experiences.

Develop a Talent or Skill Together

Do you have a skill you can teach your grandchild or a shared interest to enjoy together? If you live near one another, explore community education classes or weekend fishing or gardening shows. With a little research you can find some great options in most medium to large cities. If you don't live close to each other, you can work individually on the same shared interest and when you are together you can plan something around that interest. The key is to choose a subject you both enjoy.

- Take a baking class and then make cookies or cupcakes. Give some to neighbors or shut-ins. Go to a cooking class and work together to make a meal for a single mom who is struggling.

- Go to a gardening show and then plant a garden together. Care for the garden together and bless others with the harvest.

- Learn how to knit, crochet, or sew, and make blankets for a hospital or shelter.

- Take a woodworking class and work on a project together that can bless a family or the church.

- Take a web design class and create a website together for a nonprofit ministry.

- Learn how to take photographs and offer to provide free family photos or graduation photos.

- Be creative. Think of skills you could share with your grandchildren or research classes you can take together. The best way to encourage your grandchild to serve is by being a good example.

Take a Mission Trip Together

Going on a mission trip together provides an opportunity to bond with your grandchild in a unique and special way while serving Christ, sharing the Gospel, and making an impact on others. Children often make life-changing decisions on mission trips that impact them for the rest of their lives and may be a catalyst for serving in ministry full time. Churches are increasingly offering family mission trips, which creates an opportunity for grandparents to serve with grandchildren. If your church does not offer a family mission trip, consider coordinating one. If your church regularly offers mission trips, invite a grandchild to join you on an age-appropriate trip. What you need to do:

- Determine whether or not a trip is age-appropriate for a grandchild.

- Talk to parents before mentioning anything to your grandchild. You don't want him to get excited and then have his parents tell him he can't go or they don't have the money to send him. Offer to cover some of the financial cost if that is helpful for the family.

- Find out what needs to be done in preparation: supply list, shots, passport, training sessions.
- Read about the state or country, its culture and customs, and the mission or missionaries you'll be helping.
- Ask about specific tasks you'll be doing. Find out how your grandchild can be involved, such as by sharing a testimony, helping lead worship, or providing a devotional.
- Plan to communicate with parents while you're on the mission trip.

Ken Del Villar, a grandfather, recently had the opportunity to go on a mission trip with his grandson and offers five reasons why he recommends that you go on a mission trip with your grandchild:

1. I had the opportunity to put my spoken words into action. I tell my grandchildren that missions are important to God and a command in Scripture. During the trip, I was able to put what I had been saying into action.
2. We had a special time to build a stronger, more intimate relationship. Experiencing a mission trip with all its unique challenges allowed us to strengthen our bond. We share memories that are ours alone.
3. I had time to challenge, encourage, and build my grandson up in the Lord. He saw he could do more than he thought he could do, through Christ. He was encouraged to move outside his comfort zone, while also having a grandparent there to help, a familiar trusted face amid much that was unfamiliar.
4. We had a blessed time doing devotions together, along with debriefs each day discussing how God was working

and moving. I was blessed to hear how God was speaking to the grandchild on the trip. My grandchild was blessed to hear how God was working in my life.

5. God used us for the good of others and for His glory. Seeing friendship begin between my grandchild and an orphan at the home was heartwarming and wrenching, so much in common yet so much different. No matter how young or old, God will use His willing servants to accomplish great things for Him. Whether we were building a wall or sharing the Gospel, God was working through us to accomplish His will.

Begin praying today that God will give you opportunities to serve with your grandchild.

8

Relationship Building

Build Traditions Together

Traditions are important because they give us a sense of belonging with our family. They create lasting memories and remind us what the Lord has done in our life. Traditions motivate us to celebrate what matters, make us smile, create sentimental value, and have deep meaning. One way to keep your grandchildren on the right track is to make home their favorite and most exciting place to be. Traditions help us do that.

Take a moment and think about what you do with your family every year. Sometimes we've started a tradition and don't realize it. Repeated events with family often become traditions. Decide what memories and biblical truths you want to convey to your grandchildren through a tradition. Do you want to teach the real meaning of Christmas? Is it important to pass on your family and Christian heritage? What traditions will solidify special memories for your family? Choose traditions that work for your family. Here is a list of possible traditions to consider for your family:

- Attend family camp with extended family or a family week at a Bible conference each summer.
- Make cookies at Christmas to give to neighbors, teachers, church staff, and shut-ins.
- Collect gift cards all year and then hand them out to the homeless or families in need at Christmas.
- Share a verse at Thanksgiving dinner. Have a family football game in the yard.
- Send a letter to a grandchild when she trusts Christ, when she starts a new school year, or when she reaches a goal.
- Celebrate spiritual birthdays. (See segment on spiritual birthdays.)
- Go on a trip with a grandchild when he reaches a certain age. One grandpa and grandma go on a trip to a national park with their grandchildren when they turn 13. This is one-on-one time between grandparents and grandchild.
- Plant a tree or flowers with grandchildren each spring.
- Interview grandchildren before they start each school year. Take their picture in the same place each year.
- Design your own holiday, a day to show appreciation to each other, to celebrate the birth of a Bible character, national donut day, or anything else you want to celebrate.
- Invite grandchildren to your house every summer during your church's vacation Bible school or other summer program.
- Rent a block of hotel rooms or a big house that your family can stay in and do this every year or every other year, based on what you can afford. You pay for the housing and ask your children to pay for travel costs. Choose a fun location, a warm climate, or something on a lake or beach, and your children and grandchildren will begin to look forward to the tradition of gathering at this special location.

- Go fishing together on the opener, stay up late to go shopping on Black Friday, get a pumpkin spice latte every fall, or go garage sale shopping each summer. The options are endless.

Make an Unfinished Photo Album

Our grandchildren bring us tremendous joy! From birth to adulthood, there are many shared moments that are enjoyable to remember. Use this quick and simple idea to highlight some of the special memories with a grandchild, now and into the future:

- Purchase a 4x6 soft-covered photo album. They are available at retailers such as Walmart, large craft stores, or dollar stores. These flexible photo albums are durable and appropriate for young children to look through and play with, yet small enough for older grandchildren to put in a backpack or purse.
- Print photos of yourself and your grandchild throughout his or her life. Consider including his or her birthday or adoption day, holidays, special milestones, and everyday moments. Write the date and place of the photo on the back of each print.
- On the first page, write a note to your grandchild letting him know how much you value the memories that God has given you together, that you love him, and that God loves him too.
- Arrange the photos in the album chronologically from the grandchild's birth or adoption to the present. Leave multiple pages empty at the back of the album for future photos to be added to the book.
- Give your grandchild printed photos to add to their book at regular intervals. Consider utilizing photo printing websites such as Shutterfly or Chatbooks to automatically

sync with your phone's camera and send printed photos to you on a monthly basis.

- Optional embellishments: Decorate the album cover with your grandchild's name. Use their favorite colors or styles. Use craft paper, cut to 4x6 size, and write Bible verses, blessings, or cherished memories from the photos for your grandchild.

Send Unusual Mail

Children enjoy the surprise of opening the mailbox to find a letter or package with their name on it. Mail gives us an opportunity not only to create excitement for our grandchildren, but also to encourage and offer advice to them.

- Send mail to remind grandchildren to put Christ first and make decisions based on God's Word.
- Write your grandchild a letter when they go off to college. It will be the first letter they receive in their campus mailbox.
- For younger children, a simple hello along with a Scripture verse in an envelope is plenty!
- Get creative with what you send!
  » A ball. Write your grandchild's name and address with a marker so it's legible. Send a beach ball, which can easily deflate, or send a heavier bouncy ball or a soccer ball. Write a note on the ball or include one in the box that says, "Sometimes life bounces us around. Remember God loves you, and I love you too."
  » A Frisbee. Write a message on the frisbee such as, "I'm looking forward to playing Frisbee with you! See you soon! 2 Timothy 1:4, "I long to see you, that I may be filled with joy."

» Candy. Send a jar of candy or a single candy bar with the message, "How sweet are your words to my taste, sweeter than honey to my mouth!" (Psalm 119:103)

» A jar of sprinkles with a note saying, "Every day I thank the Lord for the privilege of being your grandparent. I am excited for your visit! Bring the sprinkles with you and we will decorate a cake!"

» A letter from the dog or cat. Send your grandchild a letter and include pictures, clippings from the newspaper, or a funny note all on behalf of your pet. Decorate the envelope with stickers and bright colors.

• If you have a question about whether or not you can mail something, stop by your local post office and ask for their suggestions. Ask if they have any tips for packaging fragile items.

• When shipping a large or fragile package, send the tracking number to your adult child so they can plan in advance for its arrival.

Celebrate the Start of a New School Year

• Pray with your grandchildren over their upcoming school year. Ask them for their prayer requests.

• Prior to the first day, take grandchildren shopping for school supplies or a new back-to-school outfit or shoes.

• Ask about upcoming athletic games, music concerts, or special celebrations. Put those dates on your calendar and plan to attend.

• Get involved at their school or homeschool activities. Volunteer to read aloud in their class. Monitor the lunchroom or halls at school or co-op. Join a Moms In Prayer group or a Grandparents @ Prayer group to pray over their education. Chaperone a field trip. Offer to teach a specific subject or unit for homeschool children. Offer to drive grandchildren to school so they don't have to take the bus. Make yourself available to help with seasonal classroom projects and parties.

- Talk with your grandchildren about school. Ask questions to learn about their school experience: What grade are you in? What is your classroom like? Who are your teachers? What is your favorite subject? What do you eat for lunch? Who are your friends? What is something you are excited to learn this year? What sorts of field trips and activities will you be participating in this year? Questions for older grandchildren: Where are you going to college? What is your major? Will you live on campus or off campus? Will you have a car or utilize public transportation? How often will you come home to visit? How can I support you?

- Meet them at the end of the first day with a special treat to celebrate.

Rubber Band Fight

If you are looking for a memorable experience, purchase a bag of rubber bands and surprise your grandchild by telling him that you are going to have a rubber band fight. Use rubber bands that are medium sized, as they fly farther and straighter, but still don't hurt. For the most fun, use an entire floor of your home so you can hide and run from one another. If you really want to introduce an experience your grandchild will never forget, purchase a strobe light and turn it on during the rubber band fight. The brief periods of dark make the rubber band fight even more exciting! Invite your grandchild over for the strobe light, rubber band fight and let the fun begin. Note: If your grandchild has epilepsy, do not use a strobe light because it can trigger a seizure.

Backyard Camping

If there is one thing most children love to do, it's camping! Combine a sleepover with some fun and adventure and it is a perfect recipe for a great time with a grandchild. Plan a yearly backyard campout and watch it become a highly anticipated tradition.

- Borrow or purchase a tent. Any tent will work, but consider a six- to eight-person quick set-up tent, which is large enough for multiple children and tall enough for adults to walk inside without bending over.
- For the best night of sleep, utilize a cot. It can get cool at night, so make sure grandchildren have enough blankets.
- Cook hot dogs and s'mores over a bonfire and place some snack foods out so grandchildren can eat when they are hungry.
- Plan some fun activities, such as yard games, football, or soccer; have a BB gun shooting contest, and play a board game in the tent.
- Read the Bible and pray before bed.
- In the morning, cook breakfast over the fire.
- Expect that grandchildren may not quickly fall asleep and may wake up abnormally early due to excitement. Don't scold them, but provide gentle guidance regarding your expectations.
- Have a Nerf gun war. See below for specific details.
- Be intentional with your extended time with grandchildren at the campout. Sing a couple of worship songs around the bonfire. Share your testimony or a way that God has been working in your life lately. Invite a grandchild to read a Bible passage and share a short devotional. Discuss biblical manhood or biblical womanhood from Genesis 2:15–18. Sally Michael's book *God's Design*, with its short devotionals on manhood and womanhood, may

be helpful. Plan some of the campout activities around a short devotional.

Nerf Gun War

A Nerf gun war is customizable to the number of people available, with as few as two or as many as you can gather. Nerf guns are sold at most big box stores, such as Target or Walmart, and can be purchased online. Check with your child to make sure they are supportive of a Nerf gun war. If your grandchild already has a Nerf gun, invite him or her to bring the gun and ammo. To get started you will separate into two teams. Try to balance the skill level and ages. Require that grandchildren stay in the yard and not go into buildings during game time. Remind all participants that the point is fun. If there is a wide spectrum of ages, it is helpful to remind the older grandchildren not to be overly competitive. Players are out when they are hit by a bullet and should hold their gun up to signify to all others that they are out. Choose the game you will play, explain the rules, and have fun! Here are five games you could consider:

- *Last Man Standing.* It's every man or woman for themselves. The goal is to eliminate all others and be the last person alive. This game is a great option if you only have a few people.
- *The Fox and the Hound.* Choose one or two people to be the fox and the rest will be hounds. Give the fox a few minutes to hide. Make sure that the hounds cannot see the fox hiding. Set a time limit of three to five minutes for the game, depending on the size of your playing field and number of foxes. The hounds try to find and shoot the fox before time expires. The fox tries to survive until time expires.
- *El Presidente.* Each team will choose one team member to be the president. The game is over when the president is

shot. The president can only have one bullet for the entire game and should remain anonymous to the other team until shot. Part of the fun is trying to figure out whom to target. All other players are bodyguards.

- *Capture the Flag.* Each team tries to capture the other team's flag and bring it to their home base. The game is over when all players from one team are eliminated or the flag is captured and taken to the team's home base.
- *Medic.* This game adds a twist to Capture the Flag. Each team chooses one person to be the medic. If a player is shot, rather than transitioning to the sideline, the player sits down on the field of play. The medic can touch a player who has been shot and the player can return to the game. There are no limits on how many times the medic can heal players. If the medic is shot, he or she is eliminated, and no one can be healed moving forward.

Fantasy Football Family League

Create a family fantasy football league as a way to connect with one another and create fun family memories. A fantasy football league is easy and free. You can create a free league at ESPN or Yahoo in less than an hour. There are only a few steps: Invite team members, set your scoring system, plan a date to draft in person or over the Internet, set your lineup, and spend time together! You can have a family league with as few as six people or as many as fourteen. The ideal size is ten or twelve, but any number can work. Choose a prize for the winner, such as a special outing with grandma or grandpa or a traveling trophy to proudly display in their room.

Connect with Grandchildren via Social Media

Utilizing social media can be an excellent way to make connections with grandchildren. Interacting with your adult children on social media will allow you to be involved in the lives of grandchildren who are young or who live far away. Interacting with teens and older grandchildren on social media gives you up-to-the-minute access to them. Depending on how your grandchild uses social media, you may have very few interactions or learn every detail of how they spent their day—down to what they ate for breakfast or specially curated and filtered photos of their latest trip to the grocery store.

Common social media platforms include Facebook, Instagram, Snapchat, and Twitter. Many people use multiple formats for different purposes. For example, Instagram is a photo sharing site, while Snapchat is used for sending messages between individuals and groups. Twitter is largely used for relaying text-based information, and Facebook combines text, photos, messaging, groups, and even shopping all in one place. Ask your children and grandchildren which platforms they use and then decide which to use yourself.

As you dive into the world of social media, keep in mind the following tips.

- While it is fun to see what grandchildren are up to and photos of their day-to-day lives, social media should not be your primary means of communication. Always aim to speak to your grandchildren in person or via telephone. Text them to let them know that you'll be calling, or to line up a time to chat. This may seem unnecessary, but taking the time to text before a phone call will be appreciated.

- Do not use social media as a means to spy on your family. Engage by posting your own photos and thoughts.

- Remember that social media does not always tell the full story. Grandchildren may post photos or videos of themselves happy and full of life while inwardly they are struggling.

- Feel free to comment on or like their posts, but not every single post.
- Tag others with discretion. Tagging means to connect a person's name with a photo or written text online. You may want to ask your grandchild's permission before tagging them. When your grandchild takes a photo with you on their device, ask them to tag you!
- If a grandchild shows support for something or behaves in a manner online that you disagree with, do not comment in a public venue. Your online interactions should be positive and bring your relationship closer together. If you are feeling anxious or judgmental toward your grandchildren after interacting with them online, make the choice not to engage with them on social media.
- Keep in mind that you are not able to hear vocal inflection or the tone of somebody's comments online. Choose to read your interactions with a positive voice. Don't overanalyze.
- Everything that is posted on social media is permanent. While you may be able to delete or take down something you posted, content posted on some platforms is archived forever. In addition, people often take a picture or screenshot of the content so they have a personal record of what was posted. Speak to others on social media in the same Christ-honoring way you would speak to them if you were conversing in person.
- Refrain from posting content that will alienate your grandchildren. Consider the perspective of your family when it comes to controversial issues before posting. It is more valuable to have healthy relationships than to let your opinions about topics drive a wedge between you.
- Utilize classes at your local library, community education venue, or at retail stores such as Apple to learn how to use

your devices more effectively to communicate with your grandchildren.

- Enjoy the many different ways of connecting that God has blessed us with!

Celebrate Major Milestones

Life is a series of milestones, and it's good to acknowledge your children's and grandchildren's accomplishments. Milestones in our grandchildren's lives give us an opportunity to encourage them in their walk with the Lord. Acknowledging a milestone is a way of letting grandchildren know they have done well, that their God-given talents are recognized, and that they are loved.

- Consider which milestones you would like to recognize in the lives of all of your grandchildren. Especially significant birthdays, earned awards, Scripture memorization, spiritual events such as a baptism, and academic accomplishments are all milestones worth recognizing.
- Be intentional when planning to acknowledge a milestone. Provide a thoughtful gift, write a letter on your own personal stationery, or deposit money into an account that a grandchild can access at a later date.
- Acknowledge milestones according to importance. Honoring a kindergarten graduation program should not have the same amount of significance as attending a high school or college graduation.
- Attend events when you can. If you live far away, call or video chat. If your grandchild is on a sports team or in band, you may not be able to get to every game or concert, but plan a visit so you are able to attend at least one event.
- Be sensitive to how you treat a grandchild who is regularly accomplishing achievements in music or sports in

comparison to grandchildren who do not participate in similar activities.

- Consider age-based milestone activities for your grandchildren. For example, an overnight with grandparents at age five, a summer trip with grandparents at age ten, and a mission trip at age sixteen.

Listening to Your Grandchildren

Just as the Lord is patient in listening to us when we pray, listening to our grandchildren when we are speaking to them communicates our love, care, and interest in their lives.

- Eliminate distractions when you are with your grandchildren. Put your cell phone on silent mode. Turn off the television or music in the background. Make their voice the primary sound you are listening to.
- Look your grandchildren in the eye, get down on their level, or invite little ones to sit on your lap to allow better conversation.
- Ask questions and listen to the answers. Whether their answers are short or long, allow them to finish what they have to say.
- Willingly listen to older children as they express their concerns, opinions, and views about the world.
- Keep conversations about their parents positive. Do not indulge in a conversation that's a litany of petty grievances against their parents. Instead, steer the conversation to how much their parents love and care about them.
- Take reports of bullying or physical, mental, or sexual abuse seriously. Follow up with their parents or a trusted family member if needed.
- Be willing to answer questions, especially those about God and the Bible. Children ask questions when they are

learning and discovering their faith. Answer questions to the best of your ability. If you are unable to answer as thoroughly as you'd like, tell your grandchild you don't know the answer and that you will find out and tell them the next time you are together.

- Relate to them and share your own stories when appropriate. For example, if a grandchild shares about struggling with a certain area of life, tell them about a time when God helped you overcome a similar challenge.

- Do your best to remember what the two of you talked about so you can follow up. After your grandchild has gone home, write it down. Is their best friend's mom sick? Did they have an argument with a girl in band? Do they have a big game coming up? Ask for an update the next time you see them.

- Let your grandchild know how thankful you are that he or she is your grandchild and that you'll always be there to listen, just as our heavenly Father is always ready to listen to us.

Visiting Great-Grandparents

A relationship between a child and their great-grandparent is special and something that many children never get to have. Grandparents can foster that relationship so that it develops into something precious and sweet for both the child and the adult. Grandparents are often the connecting link between our grandchildren and their great-grandparents. Great-grandparents are often homebound or living in a seniors' home and unable to visit family. Visiting them can take effort but will bless everyone involved. The Bible instructs us to respect one another, care for our aging family members, and value the wisdom of older people. It's easy to ignore our elderly relatives, especially if they're out of sight. You can help your grandchildren create a bond with their great-grandparents and care for your parents at the same time. Here are some suggestions to relate to great-grandparents:

- Take your grandchildren along to visit your parents. Prepare them for what to expect, especially if your parent is bedridden, connected to any machines, is hard of hearing, has difficulty seeing, or has difficulty remembering or recognizing people.
- Read Ecclesiastes 12:1–8 and discuss what happens to our body as we age.
- Be mindful of your attitude and the words that you say about the visit. We want our words to honor the Lord and other family members; our actions should exude the aroma of Christ and be a Christlike example to grandchildren.
- Pray for your parents while you're with your grandchildren. Pray they will know they are loved and appreciated and thank them for being a good parent.
- Share faith stories. If your parent is a Christian, have him tell when he trusted Christ. Have your grandchild do the same. If your grandchild is a Christian, but your parent isn't, still encourage your grandchild to share his or her faith. If you think your parent will react in a strong or cruel way, warn your grandchild. God has used the testimony of a great-grandchild to help an individual trust Christ late in life.
- Develop a list of questions with your grandchild to ask the great-grandparent: Where did you go to school? What's the biggest difference between the world today and when you were younger? What was my grandma like as a child? What is your favorite Bible verse? Sometimes children are shy around older people, and a list of prepared questions gives them confidence.
- Help your grandchild relate to your parents by talking about shared likes or topics they would be familiar with:

Great-grandpa played on a minor league baseball team. Great-grandma is the one who created the recipe for the marshmallow cookies we like to make together. Great-grandma plays the violin as you do.

- Encourage your grandchildren to make pictures or cards. If your grandchildren cannot come with you, have your grandchildren make a video of themselves saying verses, singing, or talking about their lives.

- Keep your parents up to date on what the grandchildren are doing: Aiden won a spelling bee. Noah loves building things. Cassie likes puppies.

Relating to Teens

Grandparents feel a lot of joy after a grandchild is born. Everyone takes turns holding the newborn, and dozens of pictures are taken. Messages go out to family and friends. A beautiful child has been born into the world! How much fun grandparents have taking the six-year-old to the park. He skips along beside Grandpa, chattering about school and his puppy and just about anything. What an honor to attend the fifth-grader's concert and hear her sing a solo. She beams with pride as she finds Grandma in the audience.

Then grandchildren become teens and they may not want grandparents around as often, conversation is more difficult, and grandparents feel inadequate.

Teenage grandchildren frighten a lot of grandparents. One grandma stated, "I don't know how to relate to my grandchildren anymore. The fun has disappeared." If you develop good relationships with grandchildren when they're little, you can continue those relationships when they are teens. Sometimes grandchildren need grandparents more as teenagers than they did when they were little. Parents need our support in keeping them on the right, Christ-centered track. If parents aren't guiding them in a good direction, a grandparent's influence is even more important.

Some grandchildren rebel and pull away from family and faith. We can't control their heart any more than we could control rebellion in our own children. We can pray, trust that the Lord knows the heart of the teen, and let our grandchild know we love her and care about her. We can promise that we will be there to listen whenever she wants to talk. If you want to relate to your teenage grandchildren, you need a loving heart, listening ears, and an adventurous spirit!

Here are some suggestions:

- Let them know you're praying for them.
- Listen to them. Teens spend a lot of time hearing other people tell them what to do and how to do it. Sometimes the very best thing a grandparent can do is simply be still and listen. Lecturing will not get you anywhere, but a smile, a promise to pray, and letting them know how much you love them will.
- Be available to talk and answer questions. Remind them of a verse they learned and discuss how it fits into their current situation.
- Recognize that your godly example is a powerful message to a teen.
- Take a grandchild to a place that interests them, such as a ball game or concert.
- Take an interest in their activities. Maybe the drums aren't your favorite instrument, but if your teenage grandson plays the drums, learn all you can about them. Listen to him play a solo and keep your comments positive.
- Be aware of plays, sports teams, or other activities that are part of his life. If he lives out of state, learn which online newspapers report the town sports news.
- Take grandchildren out to eat and talk about God, life, and their future over hamburgers and fries. Teens love to eat!
- Connect by social media. Snapchat is a wonderful way to connect with teenage grandchildren. They may not send

long messages, but a daily picture or a short message is not uncommon. Even though grandchildren may live far away, the connection can be consistent and a great window into their lives.

- Take them on a long trip for vacation, missions, or ministry. Maybe you work full-time, so your opportunities to spend time with grandchildren are limited. Build some extended time together into a trip.

- Don't distance yourself from your teenage grandchildren. Continue doing what you've always done: Pray for them, love them, listen to them, and let them know you care. You'll discover they're fun to have around.

Respect the Wishes of Non-Christian Parents

For grandparents whose desire, above all, is to share the love of the Savior with your grandchildren, it can be difficult when your grandchildren's parents ask you not to speak with them about spiritual topics. Situations such as these must be met with much prayer, wisdom, and kindness. Here are a few suggestions:

- Display a Christ-controlled attitude as described in Galatians 5:22–23: "But the fruit of the Spirit is love, joy, peace, patience, kindness, goodness, faithfulness, gentleness, self-control; against such things there is no law."

- While restrictions can be painful, a parent's wishes must be respected. Do not argue about the situation. You may not like the restrictions put on you, but arguing will not soften their hearts.

- Honor additional boundaries without question. If your children ask you not to take grandchildren to the ice cream shop or to that out-of-town park, you should honor these requests. If you have a good relationship with the parents, you may be able to have amiable discussions about ice cream and day trips. Accept and follow all of their instructions. Let them see that you are cooperating without debate.

- Speak to grandchildren about their parents in a kind, gracious, and positive manner. If a grandchild complains about their parents, rules, or restrictions, do not respond in a similar way. Never criticize parents. Simply say, "I honor your parents by respecting their rules."

- Always follow a parent's request, even if it would be easy to get away with stepping over the line. Seek to understand the intent of the restriction. Respect their requests.

- Treat grandchildren equally. While one of your children may willingly allow their children to visit you frequently and participate in any event you plan, including church programs, another of your children may have significant restrictions for their children. As a result, grandchildren may notice that their cousins do a lot with you that they aren't allowed to do. As much as possible, be creative in planning events for your more restricted grandchildren that are also fun and exciting.

- Recognize that you may spend more time with certain grandchildren than others. Be careful not to create jealousy or tension by posting pictures on social media or talking about the fun memories made with certain grandchildren that don't include others.

- Occasionally readdress the rules. As grandchildren grow, their parents may be more willing to allow the grandchild to attend church or read the Bible with you. Revisit the rules, but don't push. Be gentle and patient.

- Pray for wisdom. Exhibit the fruit of the Spirit. Do what you can to maintain a close bond with your grandchildren. Someday they will be adults and can make their own decisions. Your goal is to do what you can to develop a close relationship now so you will be ready for the day when you can freely share your faith.

9

For Your Home

Checklist for Successful Overnight Visits

Having grandchildren stay at your home can be a delightful aspect of grandparenting. Whether grandchildren are staying for one night or an entire week, keep the following tips in mind to make the evening experience enjoyable for everyone:

- Have realistic expectations. Be flexible with routines. Ask the parents for information about what bedtime looks like in their home and what to expect.
- Make a plan for when to contact parents and how often. Will you call before bedtime, a video chat, or nothing at all? Checking in may be helpful for some children or unneeded for others.
- Set a reasonable bedtime. Enjoy staying up a little bit later than normal, but don't keep them up too late.
- Enjoy a snack together, but limit sugar and drinks in the hours before bed.

- Before bed, have children brush their teeth, go to the bathroom, and change into their pajamas. Help with these tasks if needed. Be sensitive to the privacy needs of older children. Have extra toothbrushes and toothpaste on hand in case they forget to bring their own.
- Do not allow your grandchild to take a bath or shower unless you have specifically discussed this in advance with their parents.
- Be prepared for it to take a little extra time for children to relax and fall asleep when they are outside of their normal setting. They may be excited, scared or worried. Maintain a calm atmosphere, smile, give hugs, and allow them to express their emotions.
- Turn on night-lights to allow children who wake up in the night to see their surroundings and find their way to the bathroom.
- Consider using a fan or noise machine to drown out strange noises.
- Before they go to sleep, use the opportunity to read the Bible and pray with them. Go back a few minutes later to check in on them.
- A baby monitor can be helpful if you have babies and toddlers.
- In the evening, let grandchildren know what to expect in the morning. Put a digital clock in their space. Tell them what time you usually get up and what they should do if they wake up before you.
- Have a location in the living room or kitchen where phones and devices are placed before bed. One exception is that some children may use a device to listen to music to fall asleep.
- Provide a safe and comfortable space for sleep.
- Children under the age of three will require a crib or pack and play. Do not add fluffy, thick bedding, pillows, stuffed

toys, or bumper pads to cribs or pack and plays due to the increased risk of SIDS associated with these items. Instead, use lightweight blankets or blanket sleepers such as Halo SleepSack or Zipadee-Zip. If babies will be sleeping at your house regularly, consider purchasing these items.

- Keep bedding simple for older children. Cover mattresses with a pad in case of overnight potty accidents.

- If you don't have beds for everyone, let grandkids sleep on the floor or couch with blankets or sleeping bags. They will love the adventure! If grandchildren stay often, consider purchasing a travel cot that can be folded up when it is not in use.

- Look for hazards near beds, such as uncovered electrical outlets, bunk beds without railings, or cords from window blinds.

- In the morning, enjoy some quiet time together. Ask how they slept. Make a breakfast they enjoy. Savor these special moments!

Plan Grandparent Camp

Grandparent Camp is something more and more grandparents are doing—a weekend or week when grandchildren stay at their grandparents' house and have camp! This time with grandparents is especially precious to children who live far away, but can also be done with children who live close by. Grandparent Camp is a time to build memories and bond with your grandchildren on a deeper level than you do on short visits.

Planning and Preparation

- Consider whether you will be hosting all of your grandchildren at the same time for Grandparent Camp, or sibling groups from families. Spending extra time with cousins can be exciting for the children, but hosting large numbers of children at one time may be more difficult to coordinate. Do what is best for your situation.

- Select a spiritual theme for the week. This could be a Bible verse, a character emphasis, or a word theme. Order custom T-shirts with your theme or verse on them. Wear the shirts while you are out and about. A downloadable curriculum is available at Gospel Shaped Family (gospelshaped family.com) under the Store tab.

- Coordinate dates and transportation with your grandchildren's parents.

- Acquire permission slips, health insurance cards, and any medical information necessary in case of a medical emergency.

- Plan activities. Choose some activities that require a lot of energy, but also build in quiet rest times. Take into consideration the ages of children. Leave flexible time in the schedule for children to choose a few activities.

- Some grandparents plan camp the same week as their church's vacation Bible school. If grandchildren do not attend church at home, this can be an especially valuable addition.

- Purchase supplies for activities, food for the week, and any other household items you may need prior to your grandchildren's arrival.

- Before they arrive, explain the week's schedule to your adult children and grandchildren. Give them a list of anything special they'll need to have, such as a swimsuit or ice skates. Ask them to bring their Bible for Bible study. If your grandchildren don't own a Bible, provide one for them.

During Grandparent Camp

- The first day they arrive, have an opening meeting. Explain the rules and give out Grandparent Camp T-shirts.

If having T-shirts made is not in the budget, have grandchildren paint or tie-dye their own. Pray together about the week.

- Post the daily or weekly schedule with meal plans, activities, bedtime, and other details so grandchildren know what to expect.
- Study God's Word together every day. Integrate the Gospel into all that you do.
- Ask the children to keep a journal of their time. This could be an album or journal they keep from year to year or a different journal each year. Have them include their Bible study notes in the journal.
- Plan a service project. Put what you're learning in God's Word into practice.
- Take pictures!
- Eliminate screen time. Make your house a no TV, computer, or smartphone zone unless there is a program or movie the family can watch and enjoy together.
- Go on day trips to the zoo, a state or national park, or other fun locations.
- Have a backup plan. A week planned at the beach can get ruined by storms, or a hike up a mountain might be cancelled because of a grandchild's sprained ankle. Be flexible and ready to change plans if necessary.
- Close the week or weekend by giving out Grandparent Camp graduation certificates. Blank certificates can be found at office supply stores or are easy to make on the computer.

Welcome Grandchildren into Your Home

A visit to your house should be something your children and grandchildren look forward to! Most grandparents have not had little children in their homes for many years prior to their first grandchild's arrival. Taking steps to prepare your home before their visits will make them feel welcome and will free you up to enjoy their company rather than be distracted when they are around. Your adult children, especially those with very young children, will appreciate that you joyfully went out of your way to accommodate their growing family.

Infants and toddlers:

- Get on your hands and knees to see what infants and toddlers can reach. Inventory low-level bookshelves and cabinets, especially in the living room, kitchen, and bathroom. Put glassware, pet food, cleaning supplies, and electrical cords out of reach. Check for low-hanging tablecloths. Tie up window blinds. Secure a bookshelf or television that a child could pull down on himself.

- Consider purchasing a portable baby gate to block the tops of staircases, a crib or pack and play for naptime, and an infant swing or bouncy chair. These items will be useful if family visits often.

- If your infant grandchild is breastfed, prepare a comfortable, quiet place for feeding time.

- Keep basic first-aid supplies on hand, such as Band-Aids, burn cream, antibiotic cream, liquid ibuprofen or acetaminophen, and liquid children's allergy medicine. Hopefully you will not need to use these, but if medical problems do arise, you will be glad to have them readily available.

- Close the dishwasher when not in use and point knives down.

- Take an inventory of house plants. Move plants that could spill or potentially be toxic.

- Remove all choking hazards, including coins, bowls of hard nuts and candies, batteries, and small toys such as Legos.

- Have bibs on hand and simple snacks, such as baby puffs, yogurt melts, and soft finger foods.
- Make them comfortable. High chairs and boosters will make meal times easier.
- Keep an eye on your pets to make sure they are gentle with babies.

Preschool and elementary years:

- Recognize that children may not be as gentle or clean as you are. Mentally prepare for crumbs or messes in advance. Don't scold a child for making a mess. Resist the urge to spend your time cleaning while they are with you. Tend to messes as needed and leave deep cleaning for after they have gone home.
- Have books and toys available, especially if grandchildren will be staying for an extended time. Puzzles, games, wooden trains, Magna-Tiles, and Legos are durable, require creativity, and are universally appealing to both boys and girls.
- Encourage grandchildren to play close to where you are. Don't let an extended family gathering lead to children being asked to play in a different part of the house.
- Serve food on nonbreakable dinnerware. Utilize sippy cups if you are worried a child may spill his or her drink.
- Keep child-friendly snacks on hand. Before they arrive, learn their favorite snacks.
- Allow grandchildren to look in the refrigerator or pantry for snacks. Show them where their favorite snacks, napkins, and child-friendly cups are kept. Encourage them to ask for help if they can't find what they are looking for.
- Communicate boundaries for your home. Be clear where grandchildren are allowed to go and what is off limits. Clear guidelines will make everyone more comfortable.

Aim for freedom, rather than rigidity. For example, instruct grandchildren in a friendly way that Grandpa's office and your master closet are not places to be without an adult present. Keep an eye on children, but don't fixate on their every move.

- Let them know which drawers they can open without asking. Show them where you keep the paper, markers, and other items they might use.
- Invite grandchildren to sit on the couch with you or on your lap while you are having conversations with other adults. Include them as much as possible.
- If they will be watching TV or using media at your home, select in advance what is available. Get their parents' permission if you are showing a movie. Do not allow grandchildren to use your phone or tablet without their parents' permission.
- Let grandchildren know which bathroom to use. Have soap and a hand towel near the sink. If you have fancy soaps or other toiletries on the counter, let grandchildren know they shouldn't be touched. Place a stool in the bathroom so small children can wash and dry their own hands.
- Be clear about your house rules and support parents' rules. For example, if parents say only one cookie for dessert, don't undermine them and slip the child two or three.

Teen and college years

- Provide a chair for everyone to sit comfortably in your living room. While young men may feel comfortable on the floor, be mindful of young ladies wearing skirts or dresses.
- Learn their favorite foods and beverages and make them available. Show them where they are located and give them the freedom to help themselves!
- Include teens and young adults in adult conversation when appropriate.

- Ask teens if they would prefer to be included at the adult table for meals.

Grandchildren with special needs

- Make accommodations to the best of your ability so they can move around freely. Rearrange furniture to accommodate wheelchairs or crutches.
- Remember their unique diet or allergies when making food selections.
- Be aware of your grandchild's sensory needs. Bright lights, loud noises, TV screens, or sometimes just being in a new place can trigger sensory overload. Plan to remove distractions that will cause these reactions.
- Be flexible. Ask your adult child what would be most helpful for a grandchild with special needs and do your best to provide it.

Make and Use Prayer Cards

Prayer cards are a simple tool for praying with and for your grandchildren. You can make a set of prayer cards by purchasing 3x5 index cards to write on, or design and laminate your own prayer cards using cardstock or scrapbook paper.

- Count out the number of prayer cards you would like and secure them together as a set with a hole punch and ring, or have them spiral-bound at an office supply store.
- Write the name of a family member on each card. One person per card. Each day, flip the card and pray for the person whose name is on the card. Include the names of extended family members, the president, missionaries, and church leaders.

- Keep the prayer cards close to the dinner table. When your grandchildren are visiting, let them flip the card over to see who you will pray for together!
- If you prefer to purchase a set of prayer cards, Backgate Prayers offers personalized prayer card sets that sit on a handcrafted wooden block. Add the names of grandchildren and a family picture to life-shaping themes such as salvation, giftings, love of God's Word, kindness, biblical identity, growth in Christ, faithfulness, a servant's heart, protection, peace, integrity, and more. Place in a prominent place in your home so that you will be reminded to pray for your family.

Honor Grandchildren in Your Home

We want our grandchildren to know they are important to us. Proverbs 17:6 says, "Grandchildren are the crown of the aged." Do your grandchildren know they are precious to you? Communicate your love by saying things like, "I am so glad we're in the same family. I'm so glad God has blessed me by allowing me to be your grandparent and has given me the privilege of loving you." Show your love for your grandchildren by giving them a place of honor that they can see in your home.

- Hang photos of them on your walls alongside other family photos. Consider using coordinating frames and making a collage of their school photos.
- Display their artwork on your refrigerator.
- Place creations they made for you in special places, such as in the china cabinet or on the mantel.
- Use items they have made for you, such as hand-stitched dish cloths; play music recordings they helped create or eat treats they cooked for you.
- Create a permanent space for them to play, such as putting a toy chest in your living room or placing a sandbox outside.

- Place a sign outside your front door that says "Grand-children Welcome Here."

Explore Your City

Exploring your town or city can be an exciting and educational adventure with your grandchildren.

- Look for interesting details and locations about your city. What is your city known for? Are there any noteworthy or famous people who were born, died, or live in your city? Are there historical buildings or boutique shops?
- Find the best donuts, pancakes, and ice cream. Visit often!
- Utilize playgrounds, ponds, gardens, and walking trails.
- Many cities have books or literature dedicated to exploring the area. Look on city websites, at the local chamber of commerce, in a community group on Facebook, or ask at a local bookstore.
- Can't find great resources? Hop in the car, get a fun drink, and head down a road you've never driven! Make it an adventure together.

Stay Home Together

You do not need an expensive outing, a big house, or a large yard to find an activity to do with your grandchildren. Utilize the unique place where you live. Do you live in an apartment, condo, or townhouse? If so, here are a few suggestions:

- Swim in the pool.
- Play board games in the lobby.
- Hula hoop in the stairwell.
- Eat dinner on the roof deck.

- Invite older grandchildren to work out with you in the workout room.
- Host large family gatherings in community rooms.
- Play bubbles or draw with sidewalk chalk on the sidewalks.
- Play at the neighborhood playground.

Write Notes While Visiting

When you visit your out-of-town family, make the most of the visit by hiding special notes around your grandchild's room. Often a child's room will double as a guest room, and you'll find yourself staying in a room surrounded by their toys and books. Take advantage of the time alone in their space and leave an assortment of notes in many hiding places. Even if you don't stay in their room, you'll have an opportunity to place notes there. Your grandchild will love finding the notes over time after you've gone home.

- You will need index cards, stickers, small greeting cards or colorful strips of construction paper, and some markers or pens.
- Before visiting, write several messages, each on a different card or paper. Messages can include a Scripture verse, encouraging words, jokes, a cute drawing, a funny poem, or a simple "I love you." Make as many as you want, but the more you do, the more fun it is for your grandchild to find them.
- Bring along extra paper for messages you think of while visiting. For instance, you could remind them of activities you did together while visiting. "I enjoyed making cookies with you." "The walk to the park was fun." "The discussion we had about heaven was one of my favorite times of my visit."

- Hide the messages around the child's room, being careful not to invade anything private.
- Consider placing a note in a jacket pocket, in his or her Bible, under the mattress or rug, tucked into a notebook, inside a toy, hidden behind a picture on the wall, or underneath a pillow.
- Have fun and be creative! Include some small gifts, but probably not food! Hiding a favorite candy bar might be fun, but you don't want it sitting somewhere until the child finds it next summer!
- Not only will your grandchildren have fun finding your messages, but they will be excited about you staying in their room the next time too!

Share Bedtime Stories from a Distance

Grandchildren of all ages love having books read to them. Reading books to your grandchildren will create a bond of shared experiences, help with speech development, increase vocabulary, encourage creativity, and develop listening skills. While reading to grandkids who live nearby might be a regular activity, be intentional to do the same with grandchildren who live farther away by utilizing technology.

- Set up a standing date to read to them before bed. This could occur every evening or only one evening per week. Coordinate the schedule with your adult child.
- Prior to the time you are scheduled to read, turn on your device, connect it to the Internet, and make sure it has adequate battery life.
- Choose good books. The best books for little ones are those that align themselves with God's Word, promote excellent character, and are beautifully illustrated.

- Buy a copy of the selected book for yourself and another copy for the grandchild.
- Read favorite books from your childhood or your children's childhood.
- Little ones may ask to read the same book over and over again. Say yes and enjoy it with them!
- Select books from the Build Your Grandchild's Library of Good Books list in chapter 2.
- Before you say goodnight, talk about what you read. What would your grandchild do in the situation presented in the story? Ask questions about the book, reviewing the names of unusual animals, going over new definitions, and for younger children, repeating the order of events.
- Consider facilitating this activity with home-bound great-grandparents and great-grandchildren when it is difficult for them to be together.

Twenty-One Activities with Grandchildren

- Go out for breakfast and order a stack of pancakes.
- Host a spa day. Take granddaughters to have their nails painted or do this at home.
- Snuggle up on the couch and watch cartoons or a parent-approved movie together. Introduce grandchildren to Shirley Temple, Laurel and Hardy, and classic movies such as *The Music Man*, *Pollyanna*, and *Swiss Family Robinson*.
- Encourage your budding artist. Paint a picture or make ceramics at a local art studio.
- Do you have a dog? Bring it to a local dog park.
- Try a new recipe together or take a cooking class.
- Build a blanket fort in the living room.
- Order a root beer keg and invite everyone over for root beer floats.

- Take horseback riding lessons together.
- Encourage your grandchildren to take a hunter safety course and then take them hunting.
- Bring your grandchildren with you to your club or group, such as polka dancing, quilting, ham radio, jazz band, hiking, poetry reading, or step aerobics.
- Make a time capsule together. Include photos, a handwritten note, and anything special or unique you'd like to include.
- Host a family bingo night complete with a bingo wheel and prizes. Teach your grandchildren the joke, "B4 . . . and after!"
- Utilize senior memberships at an athletic club or science museum.
- Plan a family talent show. Encourage one another by rejoicing in the unique skills God has given each person.
- Surprise your children and grandchildren with a getaway. It can be anything from visiting an ice cream shop to a Disney vacation. Enjoy the look of surprise on their faces!
- Take a nature walk and observe paw prints, foliage, birds, and other wildlife. Utilize books like *The Field and Forest Handy Book*, *The Dangerous Book for Boys*, and *The Daring Book for Girls*.
- Create a list of your favorite childhood books and read them together.
- Go bowling.
- Give each grandchild $5 to spend at a craft store and then go home and create.
- Bring your grandchild with you as you run errands. Going grocery shopping or picking up the dry cleaning can become a fun adventure and allows time for conversation.

10

For Your Church

Launch a Grandparent Ministry

Christian grandparents need a vision and resources to help them
intentionally disciple their children and grandchildren. If your
church doesn't have a ministry that equips grandparents, consider
starting one. For more details about how to launch a grandparent
ministry, see the book *Equipping Grandparents*. Here are some
ideas to get you started:

- *Understand the biblical foundation of grandparenting.*
  Grandparenting isn't a fad or the latest family ministry
  trend. Grandparenting is a biblical command. If you want
  to learn more about the biblical foundation for grandparenting, see the book *Biblical Grandparenting*.
- *Identify a grandparenting champion.* This person will take
  responsibility for this area of ministry. If you are passionate about grandparenting, offer to lead this ministry.
- *Gather a team.* A team of committed individuals will be
  more effective equipping grandparents and will distribute
  the work of ministry.

- *Communicate to the congregation.* Discuss with your pastor how to communicate this ministry to the congregation. Can an announcement be made from the pulpit, or should it be communicated in a Sunday school class? The broader the communication, the better.
- *Repurpose existing events.* Build your grandparenting programs into the existing structures and events of the church, such as small groups, a Sunday school class, and a sermon series on the family.
- *Offer equipping opportunities.* On a regular basis, provide learning opportunities and resources to equip grandparents and remind them of the vision. Examples include a one-time class, family conference, grandparent seminar, or a multigenerational event.
- *Provide resources.* Help grandparents apply biblical principles by equipping them with good, Bible-based resources. Create a reading list, hand out one book every fall, or create a grandparent resource library.
- *Provide support.* Grandparents have many family challenges, and some experience deep grief and sadness over strained relationships or prodigal children. Support grandparents through a Grandparents @ Prayer group (G@P), create a Facebook page where needs and prayer requests can be posted, throw first-time grandparents a grandbaby shower. Sometimes the most helpful thing is to create an authentic environment where it is safe to share and where we listen, hug, grieve with a hurting grandparent, and pray.

Participate in National Grandparents Day

National Grandparents Day, similar to Mother's Day and Father's Day, occurs the first Sunday after Labor Day in September and provides a great opportunity to celebrate grandparents at your church. Ask your pastor to set aside five minutes during the weekend worship service to invite grandparents to stand up so they can be recognized, honored, and encouraged in their important role. Five ways to honor grandparents include:

1. Pray for grandparents during the service.
2. Recognize grandparents before or during the service with a PowerPoint slide.
3. Deliver a message or sermon on grandparenting. A sermon is available in the appendix of the book *Grandparenting*.
4. Hold a breakfast or lunch for grandparents.
5. Give grandparents a gift from the church, such as a book to equip them to disciple grandchildren or a gift card that can be used for an outing with a grandchild.

PowerPoint slides, prayer guides, bulletin inserts, a grandparent ideas handout, social media guides, and more can be downloaded for use by your church at legacycoalition.com/grandparents-day/.

Include Grandparents in Child Dedications

What can your church do to recognize the important responsibility of grandparents? Incorporate them into child dedications. Take the opportunity to remind the congregation that grandparents share an important responsibility in the spiritual life of children and remind grandparents of their biblical role. Provide an opportunity for grandparents to publicly dedicate themselves to discipling their grandchild.

- Read Proverbs 17:6 aloud: "Grandchildren are a crown of the aged." Provide a brief explanation such as, "This is a significant statement that speaks to the incredible value of grandchildren. It is not wealth, health, career accomplishments, or social status that the Bible says are the crown of our life. That honor goes to grandchildren. A crown bestows honor and represents a high position in life unmatched through any other source. This means that it is an honor to be a grandparent and it is a blessing to have a grandchild. The sacrifices of grandparenting are not to be seen as a burden. Your attitude and actions should reflect the value given to grandchildren by God in Scripture. Grandchildren are a blessing God has given you and come with a significant responsibility."

- Read Deuteronomy 4:9 (AMPC) aloud: "Teach them to your children and your children's children." Remind grandparents that God has given them an important role teaching their grandchildren the truth of God's Word.

- Ask grandparents the following question: "Do you commit to help your grandchild know, love, and serve Jesus?" Provide an opportunity for grandparents to say, "I do."

- Hand each grandparent a crown pin, a certificate, a book about grandparenting as a reminder of their commitment, or a Bible that the grandparent can pass on to the grandchild at a later date.

Participate in GrandCamp

If you are looking for a great way to spend concentrated time with your grandchildren that includes fun and faith, consider participating in or starting a GrandCamp. GrandCamps are offered through the Christian Grandparenting Network and are an adventure for grandparents and their grandchildren focused on leaving a faith legacy for the next generation. GrandCamps provide an opportunity to build memories that last a lifetime through purposeful activities grandparents and grandchildren experience together, time in God's Word discussing what it means to walk in the truth, and the opportunity to have fun together.

GrandCamps are amazing intergenerational adventures designed to transport grandparents and their grandchildren away from the daily distractions of life to a place where God can do something extraordinary in the lives of both grandparents and grandchildren. Visit GrandCamps.org to learn how to launch a GrandCamp, to see if there is a GrandCamp near you, to learn how to host a Grand Day Out one-day GrandCamp at your church, or to purchase the GrandCamp Field Guide for hosting a GrandCamp at your own home.

Start a G@P Group

The Christian Grandparenting Network, through the leadership of Lillian Penner and Sherry Schumann, created G@P groups, which stands for Grandparents @ Prayer. Start a G@P group at your church or home and begin praying for your children and grandchildren. Here is some basic information about G@P groups:

- *Purpose:* To call grandparents around the world to intentionally and regularly come together to pray and intercede for their grandchildren, children, and communities.
- *Goal:* To encourage and provide resources for grandparents to be prayer warriors for their grandchildren through the personal discipline of intercessory prayer in the battle against the enemy.
- *Structure:* G@P consists of small or large groups of people meeting once or twice a month at a designated location for an hour to an hour and a half for guided prayer and fellowship.
- To learn more about G@P groups, find out if a G@P group exists near you, or to start a G@P group, visit ChristianGrandparenting.net.

Organize a Photo Scavenger Hunt

A family photo scavenger hunt is a great way for your church to engage all generations in one activity. Each of the photo challenges is separated into categories. Each category has a different point value assigned to the challenges. Complete each task by taking a photo of your family members with the described clue. For example, for the clue, "Your family in a small space," participants could take a photo of their family squeezing into the backseat of a car. Complete at least one challenge from each category to receive fifty additional bonus points.

Gather families together at the start of the scavenger hunt. Explain the rules, the amount of time they will have, and what time they should return to church. Separate into groups with lists of clues, keeping family units together. When each clue is completed, one member from each family should text the photo to the designated person. This person could be a church staff member or volunteer organizer who will keep a master list of each team's points. At the end of the scavenger hunt, award a prize to the winning family and enjoy looking at everyone's photos. The following scavenger hunt is courtesy of Lilburn First Baptist Church in Lilburn, Georgia.

Category 1: Local Landmarks, 5 points each
☐ In front of the mayor's house
☐ Playing the piano inside city hall
☐ High-fiving a librarian
☐ Enjoying a playground

Category 2: Go Fishing, 50 points
☐ Invite someone you don't know to church.

Category 3: Out and About, 5 points each
☐ Something beginning with the first letter of your last name
☐ Your family reflected in something that is not a mirror

☐ Your family in a small space

☐ "Do what the sign says"

☐ With something that smells bad

☐ "Can you find us?"

☐ With something frozen

☐ With something slimy

☐ Your family crossing over a bridge

☐ Make yourselves appear really large or really small.

Category 4: Not a Walk in the Park, 10 points each

☐ Your family participating in a random act of kindness

☐ Your whole family taken by someone not in your family

☐ Entire family in a shower or tub

☐ Playing leapfrog with someone you don't know

☐ Make a human pyramid with another family.

Category 5: A Look in the Book, 10 points each

☐ What Jesus says we are in John 15:4

☐ A cup of this brings good rewards in Matthew 10:42.

☐ God is this in Deuteronomy 32:4.

☐ Something that reminds you of the promise God makes in Genesis 9:13–16

☐ Our faith need only be the size of this item to move mountains (Matthew 17:20).

☐ Ezekiel saw this on the ground (Ezekiel 1:15).

☐ King Solomon tells the sluggard to consider the ways of this in Proverbs 6:6.

☐ Get a picture with this before it withers (Isaiah 40:8).

☐ A picture with any animal mentioned in the Bible—must show the Bible verse to get points.

☐ Jesus' blood was shed on this (Colossians 1:19–20).

11

Holidays

A Word about Holidays

- Holidays provide an opportunity for extended time together, memories to be made, and the joy of bringing three generations together, so be intentional to utilize holidays to invest in your family and disciple your grandchildren.
- Plan ahead. Decide which holidays you would like to share with your children and grandchildren. If your grandchildren live at a distance, this will be especially helpful. Discuss the calendar and plans with your adult children.
- Families with young children may find it difficult to travel or to arrive at gatherings on time. Remember to be gracious and accommodating. Do your best to see situations through their eyes.
- Recognize that while you want to establish traditions with your grandchildren, your children also want to establish family traditions. As families grow and change it may become difficult to celebrate a holiday on the same day every

year. If changes need to be made, don't take this as a rejection, but as an opportunity to bless and encourage your adult children. For example, offer to host Christmas with Grandpa and Grandma on December 28th instead of the 25th to allow them to have Christmas Day at home with their children. It's not the date of the celebration that matters, it's the fact that memories are made, relationships are strengthened, and young hearts are pointed toward Christ.

New Year's Ideas

- Host a Year-in-Review Party. Serve appetizers and bubbly drinks! In an upbeat atmosphere, invite grandchildren to share their highlights from the previous year. Use prompts to help them remember, such as talking through the months. Look at your calendar or scroll through social media to remember what filled your days. Discuss memories from the year and ways the Lord has blessed, protected, provided for, and shown love. Give thanks to God and all glory to Him!

- Pray over the coming year and ask for specific requests. Ask grandchildren what they are looking forward to this year. Are there any changes on the horizon such as a move, a new baby, or a new school? Pray together over the year to come.

- Consider choosing a theme word or Bible verse for the coming year. The theme can be something you return to throughout the year in activities and conversations with your grandchildren.

- Invite the grandchildren to celebrate New Year's with you while your adult children go out. If you have younger grandchildren, celebrate New Year's earlier in the evening so they can go to bed at a decent time. Break out the noisemakers and 7UP for a Happy New Year countdown. Clink glasses, say cheers, and sing "Auld Lang Syne."

- Plan the coming year together. Give grandchildren a calendar for the new year that they can keep in their bedroom. Consider using photo websites to create a custom calendar with photos of your grandchildren. Ask your adult children where it can be hung. Write family birthdays, important dates, and Scripture verses on the calendar together.

- Set an audacious grandparenting goal for yourself! This goal could be measured by the amount of time you want to spend with your grandchildren, the number of connections you want to make with them, or specific things you would like to do with them. Make your goal, write it down, and communicate it to your adult children.

- Invite grandchildren to help take down the Christmas tree and pack up the Christmas decorations. Pray with your grandchild for those who sent you a Christmas card.

- Use New Year's as an opportunity to teach biblical truth. Incorporate verses that help your family plan for the year ahead, such as Proverbs 16:3; Proverbs 13:16; Luke 14:28; Psalm 20:4; and 1 Corinthians 2:9.

- Call your grandchildren or video chat with them to wish them a Happy New Year! Ask them about their highlights from the prior year and what they are looking forward to next year.

- If you live at a distance, mail your grandchildren a Happy New Year in a box. Include New Year's-themed party supplies, new calendars for their bedrooms with family birthdays and special dates written on them, and a note from you!

Valentine's Day Ideas

- Use paper, markers, crayons, glue, scissors, ribbon scraps, glitter, and paper doilies to make homemade Valentine's cards together. Teach them how to cut hearts out of paper!

Write notes to siblings, parents, neighbors, and friends expressing love and admiration.

- Use Valentine's Day to teach the truth of God's love for each of us, His plan of salvation, and how we can love others as Christ loves us. For little ones, read the book *Most of All, Jesus Loves You!* by Noel Piper.

- Whether they live near or far, write your grandchildren a note telling them that you love them and that most of all, Jesus loves them.

- Read or write out verses that speak of God's love, such as 1 John 4:16–19; John 3:16; 1 John 4:7–8; and Proverbs 17:17. Include the verses on notes you write, the outside of cards and packages, or look up the verses and read them together.

- Use John 3:16 to creatively write the word *VALENTINE* on cards for friends, neighbors, classmates, and loved ones.

> For God so lo**V**ed the world,
> that he g**A**ve
> his on**L**y Son, that
> whoever b**E**lieves
> i**N** him
> should no**T**
> per**I**sh
> but have eter**N**al
> lif**E**

- Help your grandchild write names on store-bought Valentine's Day cards for classmates.

- Prepare a simple meal of heart-shaped foods. Heart-shaped pizza, fruit, veggies, bread, cookies, pancakes, or whatever you can cut with a cookie cutter.

- Give a box of heart-shaped candy, which are treats loved by all.

- Send Valentine's Day cards or chocolates in heart-shaped boxes by mail. Call your grandchild and ask what he or she did to celebrate Valentine's Day.
- Most important, look your children and grandchildren in the eyes, give them a hug, and tell them that you love them.

St. Patrick's Day

- Use the holiday to encourage grandchildren to learn more about church history and heroes of the faith. St. Patrick was a pastor who brought Christianity to Ireland.
- Pray St. Patrick's Lorica (the "Faed Fiada" or "Deer's Cry")[1] for protection over your grandchildren:

> I bind me today,
> God's might to direct me,
> God's power to protect me,
> God's wisdom for learning,
> God's eye for discerning,
> God's ear for my hearing,
> God's word for my clearing.
> God's hand for my cover,
> God's path to pass over,
> God's buckler to guard me,
> God's army to ward me,
>> Against snares of the devil,
>> Against vice's temptation,
>> Against wrong inclination,
>> Against men who plot evil,
>> Anear or afar, with many or few.
> Christ near,
> Christ here,
> Christ be with me,
> Christ beneath me,
> Christ within me,

Christ behind me,
Christ be o'er me,
Christ before me.
Christ in the left and the right,
Christ hither and thither,
Christ in the sight,
Of each eye that shall seek me,
In each ear that shall hear,
In each mouth that shall speak me—
Christ not the less
In each heart I address.
I bind me today on the Triune—
I call, With faith in the Trinity—
Unity—God over all.

- It is widely believed that St. Patrick used a three-leaf clover to teach the Trinity: God the Father, God the Son, and God the Holy Spirit. Use St. Patrick's Day to teach your grandchildren about the Trinity. Find a clover in the grass or an image of a clover on the Internet. Show grandchildren that the clover is one plant with three parts, each leaf respectively representing God the Father, God the Son, and God the Holy Spirit. The Trinity is a challenging concept for little ones to grasp. Consider purchasing and reading the book *3 in 1: A Picture of God* by Joanne Marxhausen.
- Cook Irish stew and soda bread and enjoy them together!
- St. Patrick's Day celebrates Irish Christianity; research heroes of the Christian faith from your family lineage.

Easter Ideas

Easter is the most important season on the church calendar, so teach your grandchildren about the death and resurrection of Christ and the events of Easter week from the Bible. Familiarize yourself with Scripture and the timeline of events surrounding the death of Christ so you are able to easily communicate it to your grandchildren. Utilize books such as *Easter Studies* from SheReadsTruth.com, *Behold the King of Glory* by Russ Ramsey, and *The Final Days of Jesus: The Most Important Week of the Most Important Person Who Ever Lived* by Andreas Kostenberger and Justin Taylor.

Important events in the Easter calendar to discuss with your grandchildren:

- *Ash Wednesday* begins Lent, a forty-day season (not counting Sundays) marked by repentance, fasting, reflection, and celebration. The forty-day period represents Christ's time of temptation in the wilderness, where he fasted and where Satan tempted him. The purpose of Lent is to encourage believers to set aside time each year for similar fasting to intentionally focus on Christ's life, death, and resurrection.
- *Holy Week* commemorates Jesus' last week on earth, beginning with Palm Sunday and ending with Easter Sunday.
- *Palm Sunday* is the Sunday before Easter and marks the first day of Holy Week. On this day, we celebrate that Jesus entered Jerusalem as Savior and King. He was riding a donkey and a large crowd gathered, laid palm branches across the road, and shouted "Hosanna to the Son of David! Blessed is he who comes in the name of the Lord! Hosanna in the highest heaven!" For more about the event, read Matthew 21:1–11.
- *Maundy Thursday* is the Thursday before Easter when Jesus celebrated His final Passover meal with the disciples, washed their feet, and when Judas left to betray Jesus.
- *Good Friday* is the Friday before Easter, when we remember the death of Jesus, His incredible sacrifice, and when He was placed in the tomb. The Bible provides hourly details about the events of the day.
- *Easter Sunday* is our celebration that Christ is risen!

Activities

- Attend an Ash Wednesday service or host a Passover Seder meal. Set aside time to discuss the symbolism of the event and pray with your grandchildren.
- Dye Easter eggs together, or for less mess, use an Egg-Mazing Easter Egg Decorating Kit. Explain that eggs represent new life and are symbolic of new life in Christ because of His death and resurrection.
- Make a mini resurrection garden together. Resurrection gardens are simple to make and only require a few ingredients: a shallow pot, rocks, sticks, potting soil, and grass seed. Pinterest explains how to make this meaningful project that will be a daily reminder of the true meaning of Easter.
- Purchase grandchildren a special shirt or outfit for Easter Sunday. Many girls love new dresses, tights, headbands, or sparkly shoes! Consider neckties, suspenders, polo shirts, or hats for boys. Ask your children for sizes and style preference, or even better, take your child shopping and make it a fun outing.
- Attend Good Friday or Easter services together. Be willing to attend your grandchild's home church.
- Make Easter bonnets or flower crowns with your daughters and granddaughters. Craft stores and dollar stores carry faux flowers, floppy hats, and inexpensive headbands. Remove faux flowers from their stems and glue them to hats or headbands using a glue gun. Wear them to church on Easter Sunday or at your family gathering.

Easter Sunday

- Attend church together. Bring mints or gum to give grandchildren during the service. Take a photo together at church.

- Eat a meal together. What are your traditional Easter foods? Some families prefer a homemade meal of ham and cheesy potatoes while others enjoy the ease of brunch at a local restaurant.
- Read the Bible together.
- Purchase an Easter lily and place it in a prominent place as a reminder of our new life in Christ.
- Give each grandchild an Easter basket or chocolate bunnies, with their parent's permission.
- Hide colorful plastic Easter eggs in the yard. Fill eggs with candy, coins, dollar bills, or handwritten Bible verses. Hide one golden egg with the best prize inside! Be creative with what you put inside the eggs to make the activity memorable for grandchildren of all ages. If the weather is cold or wet, move indoors.

Resources

- Purchase or make your own Resurrection Eggs. Open one egg at a time to tell the story of Easter in a hands-on way. Read the companion book *Benjamin's Box* by Melody Carlson and Jack Stockman.
- Read and play Fulfilled Prophecies in Jesus matching cards from SheReadsTruth.com.
- Listen to and sing the music from Andrew Peterson's *Resurrection Letters*.
- Give each family an EvangeCube from e3resources.org. Explain it to your grandchildren and let them take it home.
- Count down the days until Resurrection Sunday with Easter cards from crewandco.com. Each card has a Scripture verse and suggested readings from *The Jesus Storybook Bible*. Crew + Co has similar cards for Thanksgiving and Christmas, which are ideal activities to be done by telephone or video chat for grandparents at a distance.

- Purchase books about Easter for gifts and set them around your home for visiting grandchildren to read: *Bread and Wine: Readings for Lent and Easter* by Orbis Books, *Preparing for Easter* by C.S. Lewis, *The Donkey Who Carried a King* by R. C. Sproul, *Holy Week: An Emotions Primer* by Danielle Hitchen, *On That Easter Morning* by Mary Joslin, *Grandfather's Story* by Mervin Marquadt, *The Bread and the Wine: The Story of the Last Supper* by Denise Ahern.
- Buy a bag of jelly beans and let grandchildren eat one color at a time while you read them "The Jelly Bean Prayer."[2] If you live at a distance, print out or write the poem and mail it with jelly beans to your grandchildren.

The Jelly Bean Prayer

Red is for the blood He gave,
Green is for the grass He made.
Yellow is for the sun so bright
Orange is for the edge of night.

Black is for the sins we made,
White is for the grace he gave.
Purple is for his hour of sorrow.
Pink is for our new tomorrow.

A bag full of jelly beans is yummy to eat,
It's a picture, a promise, a special treat,
To help us remember Jesus' work complete,
Gives us hope beyond any earthly sweet.

Ideas for Spring

- Celebrate the last day of school. Meet your grandchildren at the bus stop or their home and celebrate with a special treat or trip to the ice cream shop.
- Visit a local nursery or farmer's market. Plant annual flowers in your garden, planters, or window boxes. Build a fairy garden.

- Pull weeds and prepare landscaping for summer at your home or the home of your adult children.
- Invite grandchildren to help with yard work such as cleaning out landscaping and laying fresh mulch.
- Enjoy March Madness. Fill out a family bracket and award a prize to the winner.
- Spring clean together. Use multipurpose, nontoxic cleaners such as Thieves to allow the tiniest hands to help.
- Visit a farm or petting zoo that has baby animals.
- Host a Cinco de Mayo party. If your grandchildren live far away, send them taco shells, spices, and everything else they need for their own celebration.

Memorial Day Ideas

- Memorial Day is set aside to remember the lives of men and women who died while serving in the United States military. Explain the significance of Memorial Day to your grandchildren.
- Tell stories and show photos of family members who have served in the military. If you served in the military, share your experiences.
- Visit a historic cemetery and leave flags or wreaths on the graves of fallen soldiers.
- Give your grandchildren a red poppy to wear in remembrance of those who have died.
- Invite your grandchildren to help you hang a flag in your home.
- Pray together. Remember families who are grieving the loss of a loved one on Memorial Day. Pray for our nation's leaders. Thank God for our freedoms.
- Enjoy the day together! Have a barbeque, get outside, and be together.

Mother's Day and Father's Day Ideas

- Teach your grandchildren the biblical principles of honoring and respecting their parents. Read and discuss these verses:
  - » Proverbs 23:22: "Listen to your father, who gave you life, and do not despise your mother when she is old."
  - » Proverbs 1:8–9 (NIV): "Listen, my son, to your father's instruction and do not forsake your mother's teaching. They are a garland to grace your head and a chain to adorn your neck."
  - » Exodus 20:12 (NIV): "Honor your father and your mother, so that you may live long in the land the Lord your God is giving you."
- Teach your grandchildren the history of Mother's Day and Father's Day.
  - » Mother's Day was the vision of Anna Jarvis and Anna Marie Reeves as a way to honor mothers and show appreciation for all they had done for their children. The Mother's Day tradition began by providing carnations for ladies at Anna Jarvis's church. Women wore a different color flower to signify if their mother was living or dead. Some churches still maintain this tradition. In 1908, Anna Jarvis petitioned the president to set aside a day for mothers. President Woodrow Wilson signed a resolution in 1914 declaring the second Sunday in May as Mother's Day.
  - » Father's Day began in the United States when Sonora Louis Smart wanted to honor her father. Sonora was listening to a Mother's Day sermon in 1909 and wondered why there couldn't be a Father's Day. Her mother died young and her father lovingly raised six children on his own. Following Anna Jarvis's example, Sonora began a campaign to establish Father's Day. Slowly the

idea of Father's Day spread across the country. In 1916, President Woodrow Wilson approved a national day to celebrate fathers, but it wasn't until 1966 that President Lyndon Johnson delcared the third Sunday in June as the official observance.

- Resist the desire to make Mother's and Father's Day holidays that revolve around grandparents. Help grandchildren show love and honor to their parents.

- Prior to Mother's Day or Father's Day, ask your grandchildren if they need help purchasing or making a gift for their parents. This is especially important if your grandchild is being raised by a single parent. A few gift ideas include:

  » A handwritten card or letter
  » Favorite food items or flowers
  » A framed photo
  » An activity for the two of them to do together
  » A special dinner celebration either at a restaurant or your home

- Affirm your adult child's hard work and strengths as a parent with a call, text, or card. Be specific about the things you see them doing well. Recognize big and small things, which will be an encouragement to them.

- Go to church together. Have a corsage or lapel flower made from a local florist for them to wear.

- Pray for your adult children with your grandchildren present.

- Consider using this season of Mother's Day and Father's Day to bless your children with a gift that will encourage them in their parenting, such as a book or gift certificate for dinner as a couple. Help them with a family need, such as a new kitchen appliance or home repair.

- Be sensitive to your children and grandchildren who are hurting on Mother's Day and Father's Day. Abuse, divorce, death, or strained relationships can amplify feelings of abandonment, hurt, or loss. Show your grandchildren that you love them and point them toward their heavenly Father who is perfect, loving, and will never leave or forsake them.

Summer Vacation Ideas

Be intentional with summer months, as children have greater flexibility with their schedule and extended time away from school. Make the most of each summer by establishing a plan to engage with each grandchild in a meaningful way.

- Spend time with grandchildren. If they live far away, offer to meet their parents halfway and bring them home. Stay at a grandchild's home or invite them to stay at yours while their parents are out of town.
- Go to the beach or pool, an amusement park, a baseball game, golfing, or garage sale shopping. Go fishing and eat your catch for dinner.
- Sign your grandchildren up for Vacation Bible School. Volunteer in their classroom.
- Picnic or camp in the backyard. Play checkers or chess outside. Go for a bike ride in your neighborhood.
- Pick strawberries, raspberries, or blueberries at a U-pick farm.
- Teach grandchildren how to fly a kite or to play classic playground games such as foursquare, tag, dodgeball, kick the can, or double Dutch.
- Watch fireworks, a sunset, or a movie at a drive-in theatre.
- Enjoy a summer treat together, such as ice cream, root beer floats, lemonade, s'mores, corn on the cob. Make homemade ice cream and let grandchildren choose the flavors or toppings.

- Attend a local parade or a free outdoor summer concert in the community.
- Break out the hoses and sponges and wash the car together.
- Write a blog together to journal your adventures! There are many blogging sites, such as Medium, Blogger, or WordPress, that are free and user friendly. Set up the account and take turns writing your stories together. At the end of the summer, print the blog as a memory book.

Fourth of July Ideas

- Attend a local parade together.
- Go see fireworks together. Bring snacks, drinks, and glow sticks for the kids.
- Decorate a cake with strawberries, blueberries, and white frosting so it looks like an American flag.
- Take a country drive to appreciate the beauty of America.
- Wear red, white, and blue as a family and take a picture.
- Teach grandchildren that America was founded on Christian principles. Read a short biography about George Washington, John Adams, or other figures prominent in the founding of America. Visit providencefoundation. com for resources such as *America's Christian History, America's Providential History, Apostle of Liberty: The World-Changing Leadership of George Washington,* and *Abraham Lincoln's Faith.*
- Read all or parts of the Declaration of Independence. Find a reproduction of the original document to see the signatures of the original signers and their handwriting.
- Read *The Fourth of July Story* by Alice Dalgliesh.
- Listen to patriotic music. Teach grandchildren the lyrics to a song or make a playlist of music for the day's events,

such as "The Star Spangled Banner," "God Bless America," "Battle Hymn of the Republic," "America the Beautiful," "God Bless the USA," "This Land Is Your Land," "Yankee Doodle Dandy," "America (My Country, 'Tis of Thee)," "The Stars and Stripes Forever," and other music by John Philip Sousa.

Ideas for Fall

- Carve or paint pumpkins. Roast and eat the pumpkin seeds.
- Rake a pile of leaves and jump in. Take photos in the leaves to capture the memory.
- Spray paint a football field in the yard and play a game of flag football with family.
- Visit an apple orchard or pumpkin patch. Take a wagon ride through the fields. Let grandchildren pick their own pumpkins or apples.
- Have a bonfire in the backyard. Don't forget the s'mores!
- Invite grandchildren to spend time with you while you work in the yard and garden. Prepare plants for winter and remove dead plants. Clean rakes and shovels for winter storage. Plant fall mums in your planters. Wash and store outdoor cushions. Plant bulbs.
- Collect brightly colored leaves and make some crafts with them. Look on Pinterest for ideas.
- Invite grandchildren to help you can vegetables. Young ones can clean jars, chop produce, and measure spices. Be intentional with the time together and make it enjoyable.
- Invite your family over to watch a football game and provide good snacks.
- Make simple, delicious-smelling apple cider to greet your grandkids when they arrive at your home. In a large pot

or Dutch oven, combine one gallon of store-bought cider, two cinnamon sticks, and three sliced oranges. Let the flavors warm on the stove for about an hour. Serve warm (check temperature before serving) with your favorite fall snack, such as caramel apples or popcorn.

- Take a fall walk, enjoy the colorful leaves, and discuss what God has been teaching you and your grandchild.

Halloween Ideas

- Discuss with your adult children their personal conviction about Halloween and how they would like to approach the day with their children. Some families like to go trick-or-treating and participate in Halloween, while others don't feel it is appropriate or honoring to God. Wherever your adult children land on the spectrum, respect their wishes and seek to find meaningful ways to connect with your grandchildren during this season.

- Teach grandchildren about All Saints Day, a celebration held by the early Christian church for the solemn remembrance of martyrs. Utilize *Family Worship for the Reformation Season* by Ray Rhodes.

- Be sensitive to children and their fears. Stay away from showing images, playing tricks, or any activity that would cause unnecessary anxiety for a child.

- Make treat bags with candy and encouraging notes to deliver to friends, neighbors, teachers, and pastors the week of Halloween.

- Watch *It's The Great Pumpkin, Charlie Brown*.

- Prepare Gospel tracts or print encouraging Bible verses to hand out to trick-or-treaters.

- Plan a fun family costume-themed party. Coordinate with your adult children. Invite family members to dress up as a favorite Bible character or story, the cast of a movie, a character from their favorite book, or even groups of food.

- Before heading out for the evening festivities, eat dinner together. Try soup, mac and cheese, and fresh bread.
- Help grandchildren get into their costumes before going trick-or-treating.
- Take a family photo in costumes.
- Go trick-or-treating with grandchildren or offer to stay home and hand out candy while the children go out with their parents.
- Attend a church-sponsored event such as a trunk-or-treat or harvest party.

Thanksgiving Ideas

The celebration of Thanksgiving is an excellent time to pour into your grandchildren. Often, extended family gatherings occur and the day passes quickly without taking time to personally connect with grandchildren or intentionally pass on faith in Christ. The following Thanksgiving ideas are divided into four categories: teaching, crafts, activities, mealtime, and food. Evaluate your current Thanksgiving traditions and determine how you can better use Thanksgiving to make lasting memories and build the faith of your family.

Teaching

- Read Scripture together that focuses on giving thanks to God, such as Psalm 92; 1 Corinthians 15:57; and Ephesians 5:20. Discuss the goodness of God.
- In the days or weeks leading up to Thanksgiving, help your grandchildren write notes of thanks to their pastor, teachers, mayor, or others who serve their family in the community.

- Gather books about Thanksgiving. Read aloud Louisa May Alcott's *An Old-Fashioned Thanksgiving* and *The Thanksgiving Story* by Alice Dalgliesh. *The Thanksgiving Book* by Laurie C. Hillstrom is a wonderful resource with many historical documents, stories, and poems your family will enjoy.

Crafts

- Make a turkey using Oreos and candy corn. Purchase Double Stuf Oreos, candy eyes, candy corn, and white icing. Leaving the Oreo together, push the candy corn between the cookie layers, creating a fan of candy corn. Use drops of icing to attach the candy eyes to the flat surface of the cookie.
- Trace your grandchild's hand on paper and have them color it in, making the shape of turkey feathers.
- Make a Thanksgiving-themed paper chain. Cut colorful construction paper into 1- by 8-inch strips, enough to make a paper chain garland to fit the space you have chosen. On each strip have your family members write something they are thankful for. Get creative each year with the theme of your paper chain. Consider writing prayer requests, Bible verses, or characteristics of the Christian walk. Alternate colors and begin fastening them together by interlocking the paper links to make a chain. Choose a place to hang your Thanksgiving chain. Use it as a decoration for the dining room on Thanksgiving Day or save it until you put up the Christmas tree and use as a garland on the tree.
- When you are at Costco or Sam's Club, ask the warehouse for extra sheets of flat cardboard. Use these sheets to allow everyone to write something they are thankful for. Little ones can use markers or paint in fall colors.

Activities

- Sing together. Teach a hymn about giving thanks to God, such as "Give Thanks," "We Gather Together," or "For the Beauty of the Earth."
- Engage everyone from the oldest to the youngest in the ABCs of Thanksgiving. Start with the letter *A* and encourage a family member to say something they are thankful for that begins with *A*. Use the letters of the alphabet to remember people's names, cherished places, activities, gifts, or anything that comes to mind. Record everyone's answers from year to year. The activity can be lighthearted yet meaningful and is great with pumpkin pie.
- Watch and play a game of football.
- Run a 5k the morning of Thanksgiving.
- Volunteer to serve at a homeless shelter or food bank.

Mealtime and Food

- Begin the meal with a prayer. Consider the following prayer options:
  » A prayer of thanksgiving and blessing over the food said by the head of the family.
  » The entire family holds hands and goes around the table, each saying a short phrase of thankfulness to God.
  » Pray Psalm 136. Have multiple copies of the text available at the table. Have one person read the Psalm and the entire family say, "His steadfast love endures forever," in unison.
  » Read a liturgical prayer from *Every Moment Holy* by Douglas Mckelvey
- Cook foods that are both traditional for Thanksgiving, such as turkey, mashed potatoes, and gravy, but also foods that are a tradition for your family.

- Include your grandchildren in the preparation of the meal and table. Ask for help chopping food, making place cards, filling drinks, or announcing that dinner is ready.
- Set a festive table. Whether you choose to use your heirloom family china dishes or Thanksgiving-themed paper plates, make it special.
- If possible, serve and seat everyone at the same time.
- Help grandchildren dish up and cut their food if needed.
- Review Checklist for Successful Mealtimes with Small Children from chapter 3.
- Serve pumpkin pie and offer an additional dessert for children who do not yet appreciate pie.
- Encourage family to linger at the table rather than to get up as soon as they are finished eating. Put pitchers of water or milk on the table. Have extra napkins close at hand. If possible, serve food at the table. As host or hostess, free up your adult children to relax and enjoy their time with you. Show love to your family by serving them. Use the phrases, "What can I get you?" or "Don't move a muscle, I'll take care of it," or "Who needs a cup of coffee before dessert?"

At the end of the day, when it's time to go home, hug every one of your children and grandchildren. Look them in the eyes and tell them you love them and are thankful for them.

Christmas Ideas

The Christmas season traditionally lasts from the day after Thanksgiving until New Year's. Utilize this season to connect with your grandchildren through teaching, crafts, engaging in activities, serving, celebrating together as a family, giving gifts, and reflecting on Christ. Have fun and strive to put Christ at the center of all you do.

Teaching

- Early in the Christmas season, have a discussion with your adult children about Santa Claus and what their plans are to tell their children about Santa. Regardless of how your adult children choose to approach Santa, teach your grandchildren about St. Nicholas, the early Christian bishop who devoted his entire life to helping the sick and needy.

- Sing together! Choose a traditional hymn to focus on each year. Teach your grandchildren the words, sing it with them, and play it when you celebrate as a family. Bless others by caroling in your neighborhood.

- Explain the significance of the Christmas tree and what it represents. The tree represents eternal life in Christ. The branches remind us of Jesus' arms outstretched on the cross. Lights represent Jesus as the light of the world. The star represents the star the wise men followed to find Jesus. Gifts under the tree represent the gift of Jesus Christ. The tree itself looks like an arrow that is pointed up toward heaven. Wreaths made from tree branches represent the crown of thorns that Christ wore at His crucifixion. Angels and ornaments represent the angels who sang "Glory to God in the Highest" after He was born. Candy canes represent a shepherd's staff. Jesus is known as the Good Shepherd who laid down His life for His sheep.

- Sing the genealogy of Christ by learning the song "Matthew's Begats" by Andrew Peterson.

- Purchase a set of gold, frankincense, and myrrh online or from your local Christian bookstore. Grandchildren of all ages will appreciate being able to see, feel, and smell what the wise men presented to Jesus at his birth.

- Study Christ's birth from the perspective of Isaiah. Isaiah prophesied Christ's coming 700 years before He came. Read Isaiah 7:14; 9:6; 11:1; and 40:1–11.

- Act out the Christmas story. This is particularly fun for preschoolers. Dress up using bathrobes, use a box or doll crib as the manger and a baby doll as Jesus, and have fun reenacting the entire story.
- Read *The Legend of the Candy Cane* by Lori Walburg, which tells the story of how the candy cane represents Christ. Follow your reading with a mug of hot cocoa using a candy cane as a stirrer. This is a delightful book and activity that will be delicious for grandchildren of all ages!
- Read *If He Had Not Come* and discuss what the world would be like if Jesus had not come to earth as a baby. Discuss the questions in the back of the book.
- Display a nativity scene in your home. Purchase a Fisher-Price Little People Christmas Story nativity for little ones to play with.

Crafts

- Cut snowflakes from white paper and hang them on the windows. Use the time to teach how God created each of us individually and in His image.
- Prepare an Advent tree. Grandchildren will un-decorate the tree, one item at a time, while you discuss the meaning and significance of Christmas. Wrap tiny symbols of the Christmas story and hang them on the tree for grandchildren to unwrap. If your grandchildren visit for a short time, then wrap a couple of Advent items or one per child to open. As the children unwrap each tiny gift, explain the spiritual significance. Send an Advent tree to grandchildren who live far away and have your grandchild open each item by video chat.
- Make a garland together for the Christmas tree. Use berries, popcorn, cotton balls, or paper chains.
- Bake, decorate, and eat Christmas cookies!

Activities

- Visit a Christmas tree farm and cut down a tree for your home or theirs.

- Celebrate Advent, the season of preparing our hearts for Christmas. Purchase an Advent wreath or make your own using five candles. Help your grandchildren light each of the five candles on the Sundays leading up to Christmas. Send Advent candles to grandchildren who live at a distance.

- Demonstrate the distance Joseph and Mary traveled from Nazareth to Bethlehem. Use a map to locate a town or place that is approximately forty miles away from your home. Take your grandchildren on a road trip to the place you located on the map, stop for lunch or a snack when you arrive, and then return home. During the drive, explain that this is as far as it was for Joseph and Mary to travel from Nazareth to Bethlehem, around eighty to ninety miles. Bring a map of Israel and Egypt to show where Joseph and Mary traveled.

- Attend a Christ-centered Christmas concert at a local church, college, or performing arts venue.

- Go for a drive to see Christmas lights! Include the entire family if there is room in the vehicle. Turn on Christmas music in the car, pack yummy snacks, and stop at a local coffee shop for warm drinks while you are out.

- Watch classic Christmas movies together, such as *It's a Wonderful Life*, *White Christmas*, *A Charlie Brown Christmas*, *The Nativity Story*, and *Home Alone*.

Service

- Offer to have grandchildren work around your house to earn money to bless a pastor, missionary, or ministry with a Christmas gift.

- Find a place to serve together and bless others at Christmas. Ring the Salvation Army bell, bake Christmas cookies for homebound church members, or buy gifts for an Angel Tree.

Christmas Day

- Involve your grandchildren in Christmas food preparation. Ask them to help you set the table for dinner. Give them a role preparing food. Show them the techniques you use as you cook.
- Have festive snacks available, such as Christmas cookies, charcuterie boards, chips and salsa, crackers, veggies, and popcorn balls.
- Serve meals together at one table if possible, with everyone eating at the same time rather than excluding grandchildren to be alone at a kids table.
- Serve foods that are both delicious and traditional for your family. Pass down recipes to your children and grandchildren and teach them how to prepare these foods.
- Pray together and thank God for sending His Son Jesus to be born on Christmas to die for our sins.
- Read the Christmas story from the book of Luke. Start a tradition of serving hot chocolate and cookies as you sit together and talk about the meaning of Christ's birth. Plan the activity for a time when children can focus on the Bible and linger over their drinks rather than rush to open gifts.
- Have a birthday party for Jesus! Serve cake or cupcakes, blow out a candle, and celebrate His birth in a way that little ones can relate to.
- Invite family members to bring their musical instruments to sing and play Christmas music for each other.
- Ask your adult children when would be the best time of day to open gifts. Do your best to accommodate all of your grandchildren, even babies who need naps.

Gift-Giving

- Resist the urge to go overboard with toys. Be intentional to give gifts that will be fun as well as practical, such as tools and cooking or sewing supplies.

- Give a personalized ornament for baby's first Chrstmas.

- Ask your adult children to make a gift list for their children. If it would be helpful, have them curate their lists on Amazon.com or in a Google document.

- Make gift values equal if you have many grandchildren.

- Make it a tradition to give your grandchildren a book every year.

- Consider a gift for the entire family—museum or zoo memberships, an item they can enjoy together such as a canoe or a bike carrier for toddlers, a piano, a trampoline, or money toward something they have been saving for.

- Give the gift of paying for music lessons, swim lessons, cooking lessons, camps, or special activities they are interested in.

- Splurge and buy the entire family matching Christmas pajamas. Stores such as Hanna Andersson and Amazon sell matching pajamas in children's and adult sizes, while many big-box stores sell matching pajamas for boys and girls.

Reflection

- Keep a Christmas memories journal. Record your memories from each year, what you ate, what gifts were given, who was in attendance, and any memorable moments. Take the book out each year for grandchildren to remember the memories you made together in previous years.

Birthday Ideas

Birthdays are an opportunity to communicate affection to each grandchild. Here are some ways to make the day special and communicate your love:

- Write your children's and grandchildren's birthdays on a calendar. Upload their photos to ErinCondren.com and have stickers made of each grandchild's face for your calendar.
- Acknowledge your grandchild on his or her actual birthday. If you cannot celebrate in person, call them. Ask your grandchild how he or she is celebrating the day and affirm how much you love your grandchild.
- Send them a card in the mail. Write a note of encouragement, a prayer, and a Bible verse that you want to highlight. Include something fun, such as a small gift card, cash, gum, or a sticker.
- If possible, attend your grandchild's birthday party or family celebrations. Ask your adult children if you can help with food or birthday preparation.
- Affirm your adult children on your grandchild's birthday. Remind them how happy you are to be Grandpa or Grandma to this special child!
- Offer to host a birthday party at your house. Decorate with streamers and festive table decor. Many children are allergic to latex balloons, so talk to your child to make sure balloons are safe for use.
- For your grandchild's first birthday, give him a You Are Special Today plate from redplatestore.com. Establish the tradition of eating his or her birthday cake from this plate.
- Verbally encourage the birthday boy or girl. Have everyone take a turn sharing one or two things they love about the

child. Focus on character qualities, fun memories, unique skills, and things that will edify.

- Do you have a lot of grandchildren? Consider monthly or quarterly birthday gatherings so that everyone celebrates a birthday throughout the year.

Ideas to Celebrate Spiritual Birthdays

If your grandchildren have placed their faith in Jesus Christ as their Lord and Savior, celebrate their spiritual birthday with the same enthusiasm you would show for the day they were born. If a grandchild can't remember the exact date, then choose a day around the approximate time. Just as a physical birthday means new responsibilities and privileges, explain that a spiritual birthday encourages us to grow in spiritual maturity and continually learn more about the Word of God. Consider unique ways to celebrate the occasion:

- Plan a party! Coordinate a celebration with your grandchild's parents, being intentional to include everyone in the family just as you would with a traditional birthday. Invite friends or family. Share your testimony and encourage your grandchild to share his or hers. Invite unsaved guests to place faith in Christ.
- Gifts are an excellent way to celebrate and a daily reminder to grandchildren of the anniversary of making such a wonderful decision. Options for gifts include a Bible, a gift card to download music or a Bible app for their device, a biography about a hero of the faith, a journal to write down truths they have learned from the Bible, or a devotional book.
- Give them the gift of an experience that will help them learn more about God. Options include Museum of the Bible, Ark Encounter, and the Creation Museum. Tour a

Christian ministry headquarters or have lunch at a historic Christian college or university.

Conclusion

We hope this book encourages you to disciple your grandchildren and helps you capture those everyday opportunities to intentionally impact your family with the Gospel. As you have seen throughout this book, discipleship opportunities are prevalent, and with a little intentionality your interactions can make an eternal difference in the lives of your children and grandchildren. Don't settle for fun times or spoiling your grandchildren. Aim for more. We pray that you use the opportunities you have, whether they are many or few, to teach God's truth and point your grandchildren to Christ. Commit to obeying God by faithfully investing in the discipleship of your family. May the times with family be precious, the memories sweet, the impact eternal, the relationships deep, your years many, the fears few, the blessings abounding, and the heritage of faith in Christ one that will last for generations to come.

NOTES

Chapter 1: What Does the Bible Say about Grandparenting?

1. Josh Mulvihill, Grandparenting: Strengthening Your Family and Passing on Your Faith (Bloomington, MN: Bethany House, 2018), 70–71.

Chapter 4: Teaching God's Word and Telling God's Work

1. Fanny J. Crosby, "Blessed Assurance," 1873, in *The American Hymnal*, ed. W. J. Dawson, D.D. (New York: The Century Company, 1918), 561.

Chapter 11: Holidays

1. As quoted by James J. Walsh in *The World's Debt to the Irish* (Sainte Croix du Mont, France: Tradibooks, 2010), 70–71. First published 1926 by Stratford Co. (Boston).

2. The author of "The Jelly Bean Prayer" is unknown, and there are several versions of the poem in print and across the Internet. At least two women have been credited with writing it, at various points in the 1990s, but some parents and grandparents remember being introduced to this in the 1970s and '80s.

Josh Mulvihill is the executive director of church and family ministry at Renewanation. He has served as a pastor for nearly twenty years, serves on the board of Awana, provides leadership to the Christian Grandparenting Network, and has a PhD from the Southern Baptist Theological Seminary. Josh is the author or editor of nine books including *Biblical Grandparenting*, *Preparing Children for Marriage*, and *Biblical Worldview*. Josh's primary ministry, and greatest joy, is being a husband and father. He is married to Jen, and they have five children. Josh blogs at Gospel ShapedFamily.com.

Jen Mulvihill is a music teacher and homeschool mom to five children. She is married to Josh, and together they are passionate about training children and families to know and love Jesus Christ. Jen considers it a privilege to spend her days at home as a support to her husband and children. In her spare time, Jen leads the homeschool band she launched in 2015, sews, tends to her chickens and farm cats, and tackles DIY projects at their hundred-year-old farmhouse in Victoria, Minnesota. Jen's favorite things include growing deeper in relationship with her Lord and Savior Jesus Christ, encouraging other moms, and laughing with friends over coffee.

Linda Weddle has a degree in Christian education and is a certified early childhood educator. She has written thirteen books, including *How to Raise a Modern-Day Joseph*, and more than 2,000 short stories, articles, devotionals, and radio scripts for Christian organizations. For twenty-five years she was a senior writer and program developer at Awana and taught workshops across the country. Linda has worked in almost every area of children's ministry, including summers when she and her pastor husband taught at camps and she could tell children stories that reflected their everyday lives, teaching them biblical truths. Linda has two children and six grandchildren. Her blog for teachers and parents is at groundthemforlife.com.

More Foundational Grandparenting Resources

Dr. Josh Mulvihill helps you speak wisdom and godliness into the lives of your grandchildren. Here he gives you all you need to invest spiritually in your grandkids, from sharing with unbelieving grandkids to discipling them into a mature faith. Perfect for individual use, small groups, or Sunday school classes.

Grandparenting by Dr. Josh Mulvihill

With depth and relevance, this leadership book places grandparenting ministry on a firm scriptural foundation. Ideal for pastors and church leaders as well as for use in the classroom at seminaries, this resource is perfect for helping you show how grandparents can invest spiritually in their grandkids and speak wisdom and godliness into their lives.

Biblical Grandparenting by Dr. Josh Mulvihill

Living far away from your grandchildren is hard. But just because you can't spend as much time with them doesn't mean you can't have an impact on their lives. In this practical book, you'll learn how to make the most of the opportunities you do have to connect with your grandkids and, more importantly, how to encourage their relationships with God.

Long-Distance Grandparenting
by Wayne Rice and Dr. Josh Mulvihill, general editor

BETHANYHOUSE

Stay up to date on your favorite books and authors with our free e-newsletters. Sign up today at bethanyhouse.com.

 facebook.com/BHPnonfiction   @bethany_house_nonfiction

 @bethany_house